Richard Mounteney Jephson

He would be a Soldier!

Eighth Edition

Richard Mounteney Jephson

He would be a Soldier!
Eighth Edition

ISBN/EAN: 9783337132781

Printed in Europe, USA, Canada, Australia, Japan

Cover: Foto ©ninafisch / pixelio.de

More available books at **www.hansebooks.com**

HE WOULD BE A SOLDIER!

BY

R. MOUNTENEY JEPHSON

AUTHOR OF
"A PINK WEDDING," "THE GIRL HE LEFT BEHIND HIM," ETC., ETC.

WITH ILLUSTRATIONS

EIGHTH AND CHEAPER EDITION

LONDON
RICHARD BENTLEY AND SON
Publishers in Ordinary to Her Majesty the Queen
1890
[*All rights reserved*]

LIST OF ILLUSTRATIONS.

	PAGE
Mr. Boomershine catches the Martial Fever - - - *R. Caldecott.*	5
"Mr. Boomershine held out the recaptured Guinea-Pig as a living Apology" - - - - ,,	44
"Then let me like a Soldier Fall" ,,	145
"There, Sir, Mr. Wilder says if you take that, and have your Tub after, you'll be all right for your Drill" - - - ,,	150

CONTENTS.

CHAPTER I.

Illustrious descent of our hero—Short genealogical sketch of the Boomershines of Snoozleshire—Military genius, like murder, will out—Futile attempts to stifle it—Fortification under difficulties—Family considerations sacrificed to national welfare—The bud of youthful ardour nipped by the frost of official coldness . . . 1

CHAPTER II.

Military preparations—A council of war, resulting in a patriotic sentiment and a song—A good piece of advice, founded on Shakespeare and Burns . 10

CHAPTER III.

A military toilet—A sword dance, which includes a reel and a fling—None but the brave deserve the fair—A trusty blade 22

CHAPTER IV.

Family presentations—True generosity—Great expectations—Noble sacrifice on the part of a relative—A virtuous and accomplished bird . . 29

CHAPTER V.

Go where glory waits thee—A soldier's tear—Mentor improves the occasion, with doubtful results—He indulges in a light repast and suffers therefrom — Gone away! — Outraged modesty — Mr.

Boomershine renders himself liable to prosecution by the Society for the Protection of Women—Exciting scene—Painful separation . . . 37

CHAPTER VI.

Is an important one—Our hero makes the acquaintance of a distinguished brother-officer, and at once profits thereby. He obtains a great deal of information of a novel character—He is guilty of wholesale traduction of character, and wounds one gentleman in his tenderest point—He engages in a transaction of a mysterious nature with a barmaid, which gets him into a ticklish position, and finally results in an engagement—He arrives at Aldershot 46

CHAPTER VII.

Introduction to military life—A pleasant *jeu d'esprit*, entitled "The Sleeper Awakened"—Striking ceremony of initiation—Sub-Lieutenant Boomershine lies like a warrior taking his rest, and doesn't much like it 64

CHAPTER VIII.

First awakenings—A matinée militaire—Precept upon precept 80

CHAPTER IX.

A trying ordeal—Curious phenomenon—The terrors of martial law 88

CHAPTER X.

A terrible martinet — The correct position of a soldier—Touching instance of self-sacrifice on the part of Lieutenant Wilder—Our hero embarrasses himself with a gaunt giant in a shell-jacket—He falls into the hands of an Indian warrior and *Raconteur* of distinction — He makes a tour of inspection—The piping times of peace . . 102

CHAPTER XI.

Is another important one— Sub-Lieutenant Boomershine's first night at mess — Two heroes of romance—Disagreeable position between two fires—The pure Pierian spring—The flowing bowl—Our hero performs a double feat, and, in spite of sound practical advice from his friend Wilder, makes an enemy for life—He attends the " Symposium," and conducts himself with distinction at a performance held therein—For the last time he asks, " Let me like a Soldier fall!" and they let him 117

CHAPTER XII.

Remorse—Repentance and soda-water—Agonising doubts—Determination to desert—Breakfast and change of mind 147

CHAPTER XIII.

Is perhaps the most thrilling in the whole book—Our hero is pleased to find that he commands the respect of his brothers-in-arms — He gladdens the martial soul of Corporal Stickler—He applies a highly complimentary term to his commanding officer, with an awful result—He drives a worthy old soldier clean out of his mind, and nearly goes out of his own—He contemplates suicide—When night is darkest, dawn is nearest—Explanation 159

CHAPTER XIV.

Church parade—Pride has a fall—The church militant—A Sunday in quarters . . . 169

CHAPTER XV.

Our hero serves his country with energy and zeal—He sees much of that great man Corporal Stickler, and the more he sees the deeper he is impressed—He is eager in the pursuit of professional knowledge—He passes triumphantly through a trying ordeal, and treads the stony path of duty—He obtains " leave of absence on private affairs," and previous to his departure obeys an injunction touching the moral welfare of the benighted soldier 174

CHAPTER XVI.

Is so shocking that people of weak nerves are recommended to let it alone—Mentor becomes a painful instance of the truth of his own favourite precept—Wholesale slander—Virtuous indignation—Ingenious scheme for the regeneration of Africa—A shadow darkens the once hopeful House of Boomershine 190

CHAPTER XVII.

Return to Duty—Verisopht becomes an authority—Change of quarters—Sensation in Snoozleton—Different views of the British soldier—Aunt Millicent flees from contamination . . . 205

CHAPTER XVIII.

A distinguished veteran—A sop to Cerberus—The light fantastic toe—Our special correspondents—Eccentricities of matured military genius . . 214

CHAPTER XIX.

Is a sad one, inasmuch as the reader bids farewell to three distinguished characters—Climax of the rivalry between Captains Chutney and Calipash—Heartless decree of the Horse Guards—Affecting farewell 230

CHAPTER XX.

Tardy regeneration of Mentor—Daring trespass—Domestic devotion—The pursuit of botany under touching circumstances—Remorse—The *amende honorable* 261

CHAPTER XXI.

A *reconnaissance*—Joe Miller in regimentals—The game of war—A picture of peace—Colonel Rooteen's brain reels under a shock—He recovers—Villainy exposed—A rapid retrograde movement 276

CONCLUSION.

Satisfactory, we hope, to all concerned . . 291

HE WOULD BE A SOLDIER!

CHAPTER I.

Illustrious descent of our hero—Short genealogical sketch of the Boomershines of Snoozleshire—Military genius, like murder, will out—Futile attempts to stifle it—Fortification under difficulties—Family considerations sacrificed to national welfare—The bud of youthful ardour nipped by the frost of official coldness.

THOUGH the Boomershines of Snoozleshire are unquestionably a good family, it is collaterally, rather than directly, through them that our hero, himself a Boomershine, lays claim to a descent so highly respectable that it borders on the illustrious. His father, a quiet country gentleman of easy means, is closely related to that family of Green of which Mr. Verdant Green is so distinguished an ornament. In fact, Mr. Boomershine and Mr. Verdant Green are first cousins, so that our hero enjoys the honour of being first cousin once removed to the latter celebrated character. His mother was a Miss Simple, a descendant of a distinguished naval officer, Captain Peter Simple; and through her he can also trace his descent from the Simon family, a highly respectable, though apparently poor one. Indeed, so reduced in circumstances was its most celebrated member, that on one occasion, we are told, he was unable to command a sum of ready money sufficient to purchase the ware of an itinerant vender of pastry.

His grandmother, on his father's side, was a Verisopht, one of that noble family from which the talented and astute Lord Frederick Verisopht sprang. Mr. Boomershine was proud of this aristocratic connection, and on our hero's appearance on life's stage as his son and heir, the noble name of Verisopht was conferred upon him.

Through his father, Verisopht Boomershine is also collaterally descended from another celebrity, one John Raw, Esquire, to whom posterity has likewise accorded a niche in the temple of Fame.

Thus, in virtue of his descent, young Boomershine united in himself not only the illustrious blood, but also the proverbial worldly wisdom and tact of the Greens, the Simples, the Simons, the Verisophts, and the Raws.

Not a little proud of this genealogical combination was that branch of the Boomershines of which I write, and on their carriages and harness, their spoons and forks, their notepaper and envelopes, were emblazoned the arms of Boomershine, quartered with those of Green, Simple, Simon, and Verisopht. These armorial bearings were imposing in the extreme. There were three crests: an evergreen on a mount vert for Green: a son of a sea-cook hornpipant for the great naval family of Simple; and a pieman rampant for Simon; while, for the whole, a single motto sufficed, "Semper Virens."

As Verisopht gradually grew from a baby into a little boy, from a little boy into a big one, he developed, both mentally and physically, the many brilliant qualities of his ancestors, to the delight and admiration of his parents. Mr. Boomershine would often look at him and proudly remark that he had the "regular Verisopht head." Then, too, he had the Raw hands, the Simple elevated eyebrows, and the Green elbows; while an inordinate passion for pastry conclusively stamped him a Simon.

In the calm seclusion of his country home it is hard to understand by what means young Verisopht's soul first became fired with martial ardour; but it is supposed that the conflagration is attributable to a panorama of the Battle of the Alma, which, in conjunction with two fiddles, a trombone, and a cornet-à-piston, made its appearance in the village a few years ago.

Immediately on these flames bursting forth, Mr. Boomershine promptly converted himself into a moral fire-engine, and threw such volumes of cold water as nearly extinguished them for ever. His two eldest daughters, Fanny and Carry, however, looked with considerable favour on their brother's military aspirations, and did their utmost to fan the flames into fresh life. On the other hand, Mrs. Boomershine, as was only right and proper, sided with her lord and master, and worked vigorously at the moral fire-engine pumps.

Mr. Boomershine continued his opposition until the discovery that his son had taken to the practical study of fortification by throwing up a front of Vauban's first system on the croquet-lawn rather staggered him. Recognising in this act the true flash of military genius—a genius which, bottled up in one direction, would burst out in another—Mr. Boomershine at once decided that it would be unpatriotic to deprive the country of a future Wellington or Marlborough, and, as individual interests should always be sunk in national considerations, he gave his consent to the military scheme.

This was at first a sore disappointment to Mr. Boomershine; but he solaced himself by transferring to his second son Peter (called after the naval ancestor of his mother) all those hopes of a glorious academical career which he had hitherto placed on his first-born; and, like a true philosopher, having made up his mind to a certain course, he closed his soul to useless repining, and looked only on the bright side of the question. In this sensible frame of mind he not only grew reconciled to the change in his son's future, but even became himself so imbued with military ardour as to assist in the construction of earthworks in the kitchen garden, regardless of the taunts levelled at him by Mrs. Boomershine, who, smarting under the demolition of her celery and asparagus-beds, failed to see in a "ravelin," a "demi-flèche," or a "bastion," anything but a dirt-pie of larger dimensions than usual.

This last practical tuition was all that was required to complete Verisopht's professional education; for, having been destined for college honours, he possessed a great deal more than enough of mathematical, historical, geographical, and linguistical acquirements to enable him to pass the necessary examination; and, the usual preliminaries having been gone through, this he did with flying colours.

There was now nothing to be done but to wait until the important announcement in the *Gazette* should notify his appointment, and, in the meantime, to prevent those rudiments of a military education, acquired at the expense of the celery and asparagus-beds, from growing rusty.

Several months thus passed in anxious expectation, until at last, on a certain eventful Wednesday morning, when the family were at breakfast, the arrival of a large official envelope, addressed, "On Her Majesty's Service," to "Sub-Lieutenant Verisopht Boomershine, 119th Regiment," threw the whole household into a state of great excitement.

"The 119th! Oh, I do believe it's a Highland regiment! Oh, Verry! I wonder how you will look in a kilt!" exclaimed Fanny.

Verisopht surreptitiously felt his calves under the table, and inwardly breathed a prayer that his sister might be mistaken. Further reference to the letter proved that she was. It merely informed Verisopht that His Royal Highness the Commander-in-Chief had been pleased to appoint him to a sub-lieutenancy in Her Majesty's 119th Regiment of Foot, and further directed him to report himself at the headquarters of that distinguished corps, at Aldershot, on exactly that day two months.

Verisopht's military ardour burned so fiercely within him, however, that he at once replied that he scorned a life of inaction, and, so far from requiring two months' leave, would be at the service of his country in two weeks.

This soldier-like promptitude awakened the highest admiration in the family, and they awaited with considerable expectation the complimentary letter from the Duke himself, which they had not the slightest doubt such conduct would call forth. Indeed, the two eldest girls, Fanny and Carry, engaged in quite a serious altercation as to who should have the royal autograph for her album, until Peter Boomershine, being called upon by his father to adjudicate, with a view to exercising his powers of discrimination, wisely removed the apple of discord by awarding it to himself, in anticipation. The reply itself, however, would have settled the matter without young Peter's masterly adjudication, for it was from no royal duke—nor even general, for that matter—but from some humbler individual, styling himself an acting deputy-assistant something or other, who begged Sub-Lieutenant Boomershine to be good enough to do what he was ordered, and to join on the day previously specified without any comment whatsoever.

CHAPTER II.

Military preparations—A council of war, resulting in a patriotic sentiment and a song—A good piece of advice, founded on Shakespeare and Burns.

THE family thought that perhaps the country was not so grateful for the honour they were conferring on it as it might be; but any chagrin they felt was lost in the preparation of Verisopht's outfit. Mrs. Boomershine superintended the linen department; Carry and Fanny plied their knitting, crochet, and sewing needles with cunning and busy hands; Peter applied himself to the translation of such passages of Cæsar's

Gallic War as he thought might be of professional value; while Mr. Boomershine's part in the performance consisted merely in putting his hand into his pocket.

Of all the preparations, those pertaining to the uniform were the most interesting, and this Mr. Boomershine, being an advocate for the encouragement of native talent, intrusted to the leading tailor of their country town; while the barrack-room furniture was ordered from one of those enterprising tradesmen, under the weight of whose circulars the postman had staggered to Mr. Boomershine's door for several consecutive mornings after Verisopht's name had appeared in the *Gazette*.

This was not so exciting a department as the uniform, but still it had its pleasures. It was very inspiriting to Verisopht, and gratifying to his relatives, to see "V. S. R. S. Boomershine, Esq., 119th Regt.," written in great white letters on the cases containing the different articles of barrack furniture. It was capital fun, too, peeping into this and prying into that, and examining the compact little canteen-case, holding a breakfast service for two, and admiring how exactly everything fitted in its place, even to the two tiny salt-spoons. Then it was as good as a Chinese puzzle putting up the portable washing-stand. But the most admirable and ingenious contrivance of all was the patent folding-chair, which puzzled them more than anything else, until Mr. Boomershine practically explained its mechanism and use in a startling manner, by making a sandwich of himself between the seat and the back.

As the expiration of the two months drew near Verisopht found himself more and more the hero of the hour, and family conversation ran almost entirely upon him and his future career. Sometimes it took the form of playful banter, sometimes of ambitious forecasts, and sometimes, as in the following instance, of sound, practical advice from Mr. Boomershine.

"Verisopht," said Mr. Boomershine one evening, from his commanding position on the hearthrug, as he beamed on the assem-

bled family, "without counselling you to
follow a roystering, rollicking course of
life, I would still advise your entering into
the harmless amusements of your brother
officers, and doing so—as long only as they
continue to be harmless, mark me—with
zest and spirit. I would not, indeed, have
you as reckless and wild as your cousin
Verdant was at college; and, in truth, I
imagine the tricks he tells us he used to
play upon poor Mr. Bouncer and Mr. Lar-
kins, when he was a young freshman, would
not be tolerated nowadays in any assem-
blage of English gentlemen. However, be
that as it may, our cousin Verdant was undoubtedly popular. Certainly he was not,
as he has so often told us, a young man
easily taken in, and I recollect that, even
as a youth, he wore spectacles, which probably secured for him an amount of consideration and, I may say, respect seldom
accorded to a young man by his compeers.
Now I think, besides this, I may trace some
of his popularity to a song he used to sing
with the greatest success, ' I dreamt I

dwelt in marble halls.' Now you might, with your sister's assistance, learn some nice song which——"

Here the enthusiasm of the family led it into a very unusual course, that of cutting Mr. Boomershine off in the full flow of his oratory; and there was a general chorus of "Oh yes — how nice!" combined with a clapping of hands.

"Just the thing," said Carry. "Why shouldn't it be, then, the song that cousin Verdant used to sing? You say it was a great success, papa."

"Well, no," said Mr. Boomershine. "I should rather recommend a song embodying some soldier-like sentiment."

Peter, the "double first" in the bud, here suggested that he should translate into Latin verse "The British Grenadiers." It was hackneyed, he admitted, in the mother tongue; but in Latin, he had no doubt it would be a pleasing novelty to Verry's brother officers.

"Well, no again," said Mr. Boomershine. "There are many objections to that. Amongst others, for instance, how would you render into the Latin tongue 'With their tow-row-row-de-dowdow?'"

Peter, on this, found himself literally "au bout de son Latin." He hung his head abashed, and confessed that his father had fairly posed him. He then retired to a corner of the room in low spirits and the company of his Lexicon.

"Well, what do you say to 'Let me like a soldier fall?' Carry's got the music," suggested Verisopht himself.

"Oh yes!" "Just the thing!" "Capital!" were the exclamations on all sides.

"A happy thought indeed, Verisopht, my boy," said Mr. Boomershine; "a very happy thought. It is a song inculcating a noble and patriotic moral. 'Dulce et decorum est pro patriâ mori,' as our old friend Horace——"

Here the irrepressible Peter perked up a little, and insisted on construing and parsing the sentence for the general benefit.

"'Then let me like a so-o-o-ldier fall!'"

repeated Mr. Boomershine. And here, carried away by the grandeur of the sentiment, he struck his chest so mighty a blow that he shot his spectacles into the grate.

"'Then let me like a soldier fall,'" he repeated once more, with some abatement of spirit, as he stooped down to pick up his glasses, and simultaneously frowned on two younger members of the family, who were at that ticklish age which often laughs in the wrong place, and were highly amused at what they took for part of the performance. "I don't know that you could do better, Verisopht, than to commit that song to memory," he concluded, as he readjusted his spectacles and beamed once more benevolently through them on the two small culprits, who, having now seen the error of their infantile ways, had resumed that air of serious attention with which all Mr. Boomershine's sober remarks were received in the family circle.

On this Verisopht was forthwith borne away to the piano by his sister, and from that moment, at intervals during the next fortnight, a thin, quavering voice was frequently heard uplifted in the same noble request for a patriot's grave.

Mr. Boomershine would not have been the high-minded and conscientious parent he was had he sent his son out into the world without some words of advice on a subject deeper than that of securing the goodwill of his brother officers by mere social qualities of goodfellowship.

"My dear boy, there is a great deal of good to be got out of Shakespeare's works," said Mr. Boomershine one day, after having culled some lessons from a much greater work. "Before you leave me I wish you to commit to memory those beautiful and noble words of counsel addressed by Polonius to his son Laertes. It has sometimes struck me as incongruous, that Shakespeare should have put these sublime words into the mouth of a character like Polonius, who was a busybody, an eaves-dropper, and a sycophant; but doubtless there existed in that great mind some good reason for doing so, and I have sometimes thought it may have been meant to show how much easier it is to give good advice than to follow it, how much easier to preach than to practise. Be that as it may, the words are such as I should like to sink deep into your heart. I will repeat them to you, my boy."

Here the true-hearted and simple-minded gentleman took his son's hand in his, and with a glistening eye and a voice often trembling with emotion, repeated the beautiful lines, interspersing them as he went along with characteristic remarks of his own.

"'. . . Give thy thoughts no tongue,
Nor any unproportion'd thought his act.
Be thou familiar, but by no means vulgar.'

Remember, Verry, the old adage: 'Familiarity breeds contempt.'

"'The friends thou hast, and their adoption tried,
Grapple them to thy soul with hooks of steel—'

Mark that well, my dear boy. A true friend, Verisopht, is one of the greatest blessings a man can have in life. 'Friendship, mysterious cement of the soul, sweetener of life, solder of society !' says another poet. Yes, my boy, when you find a real friend, 'grapple him to thy soul with hooks of steel.'

> "'But do not dull thy palm with entertainment
> Of each new-hatch'd, unfledg'd comrade. Beware
> Of entrance to a quarrel; but, being in,
> Bear it, that the opposer may beware of thee.'

To this last point I have nothing to add, but to remind you that you are an English gentleman and an English soldier.

> "'Give every man thine ear, but few thy voice:
> Take each man's censure, but reserve thy judgment.'

We none of us are faultless, and bear that in mind, my boy, when the blame of your superior seems to fall harshly upon you.

> "'Costly thy habit as thy purse can buy,
> But not expressed in fancy; rich, not gaudy:
> For the apparel oft proclaims the man.'

Dress like a gentleman, Verisopht; but don't be a fop. Avoid what our cousin

Verdant calls 'loud patterns,' and don't run up a larger tailor's bill than you can conveniently pay at the end of every half-year.

"'Neither a borrower nor a lender be;
For loan oft loses both itself and friend.'

Never borrow. Come to me, and I will *give*. But, as regards the latter part of the admonition, I must be guilty of the presumption of differing from our immortal bard. Do not lend promiscuously; but if you find a friend—a true friend, whom thou hast 'grappled to thy soul with hooks of steel,' hang it! sell the very coat off your back for him if he be in penury and want. Bless my soul! what was Shakespeare about?" said Mr. Boomershine warmly. "It was not thus in the 'Merchant of Venice,' a play apparently written with the purpose of setting forth the beauties of friendship—it was not thus that Bassanio treated Antonio, and I do not think *that* loan was the cause of any rupture between that friendship; on the contrary, it cemented it.

" 'This above all——'

Yes, above *all*, mark you well, Verisopht; for beautiful as have been the foregoing lines, the conclusion surpasses in beauty all that has gone before.

> " 'This above all—To thine own self be true,
> And it must follow, as the night the day,
> Thou canst not then be false to any man.'

I would that these noble words of England's noblest poet were engraven on the hearts of every one of her sons. There are a few more words I intended speaking to you before our parting, and I'll take this opportunity of saying them now. There is no subject on which it is easier to appear smart and funny, and which so easily raises a laugh amongst the thoughtless, as a Scriptural one, treated with levity. But when the temptation is before you, remember, my dear boy, that

> " 'An atheist's laugh's a poor exchange
> For Deity offended.' "

CHAPTER III.

A military toilet—A sword dance, which includes a reel and a fling—None but the brave deserve the fair—A trusty blade.

VERISOPHT had barely perfected himself in his song, when one evening there arrived a japanned air-tight tin case with a beautiful little brass plate on the top inscribed with his name and regiment in full; and when the case was opened there was such a dazzling display of scarlet, brass buttons, and gold lace, that the younger portion of the family became almost demented with excitement. With a heart full of martial ardour Verisopht bore the case off to his room, and proceeded, by general desire, to array himself in the gorgeous trappings of his profession. His notions of a military toilet were rather foggy; but as those of the spectators would be equally so, this was of no consequence; and when he *did* make his appearance, such little mistakes as wearing his sash on the wrong shoulder, his sword on the right side, and the buckle of his stock well up the back of his head, were quite lost in the general splendid effect.

Mr. Boomershine at first looked at his family—from Mrs. B., clasping her hands ecstatically, to the baby crowing and screeching—with smiling condescension; but at last even he caught the martial fever, and, placing the shako on the top of his head, folded his arms and transfixed an imaginary enemy of his country with a bloodthirsty glare. This was received with loud expressions from the whole family, particularly the baby, who, with the vivid imagination of infancy, identified himself with the supposititious enemy, and screamed himself successively into pink, red, blue, and purple. He was fast deepening into black when he was hurriedly borne away to the nursery, there to work gradually back to his original complexion under the soothing influence of the bottle. This little episode led to Mr. Boomershine figuring in a much milder character, and, though he still absently retained the shako on his head, it was but tamely that he defended himself from Mrs. Boomershine's charge of thoughtlessness and cruelty. This was of short duration, however, and Mr. Boomershine was soon himself again.

"I was thinking," said Carry, "it would be so soul-stirring if Verry were to sing his song in his regimentals—in character, in fact, and then we could judge so much better of the effect."

This proposal was at once carried out, and it was indeed, as Carry had said, "soul-stirring," particularly about the higher notes, to hear and see the young soldier sing the noble song, with one hand on the hilt of his sword and the other resting on his bosom.

Mrs. Boomershine and her daughters were almost affected to tears, and Mr. Boomershine himself left off his pantomimic accompaniment to whisper in Mrs. Boomershine's ear his firm opinion that that song would at once raise Verry to quite a dizzy height of popularity amongst his comrades. At the conclusion of the performance Verisopht blushingly received the tributes of praise showered upon him. Mrs. Boomershine said it was touching and noble; Carry that it was lovely; Fanny, heavenly; and so forth.

"Oh, let's have a dance, Verry," now suggested the volatile Fanny. "I should *so* like to know what having an officer's arm round one's waist feels like."

Mr. Boomershine gently chid the foolish girl; but not offering any serious opposition to her harmless proposal, she started off with Verry to the tune of the Copenhagen waltzes, which were considered rather new ones down in the Boomershines' part of the world.

For a few turns Verisopht acquitted himself with his usual primitive grace; but after that he suddenly executed a figure which his sisters had not included in his dancing lessons. Indeed, I believe it is never taught, and will therefore give it in full. It must be danced with a sword on, and mainly consists in getting that weapon between the feet, and then bringing the back of your own head and that of your partner into smart contact with the floor or the nearest piece of furniture, at the same time displaying the soles of your dancing-shoes to the company. It is not a difficult figure by any means, and requires *no* practice. Indeed, only get the sword into the required position, and the remainder will follow with charming spontaneity.

Having thus distinguished himself, Verisopht proceeded, by special desire, and escorted by all his brothers and sisters, to the servants' hall. Here he was received with unbounded enthusiasm and eulogistic stage whispers. The cook said to the coachman, "Didn't he look sperritted just?" The coachman replied to the cook that she might "say that, and 'andsome as well, without tellin' a lie." The gardener kept on vaguely asking, "Who'd a thought it now?" The footman, who was a "lady's man," or rather a lady's "lady's" man, said he looked "quite the gay Lathero;" Matilda said, "Lawks!" Jane improved on Matilda with, "Goodness gracious me, oh, lawks!" and Susan, the scullery-maid, if low, was still sincere, with "Jimini Cracks!" The only one who was silent was Buttons: his heart was too full to speak—full of a resolve to enlist as soon as he had sufficiently elongated himself.

This was all very trying to Verisopht, and after a few moments he found it rather hard to keep the character going, until, drawing his sword with a flourish, he regularly brought down the house, particularly that lath and plaster portion of it immediately over his head. Encouraged by the success of this line, he gave them something else in the same style, and, with a vigorous cut at what was intended for an imaginary enemy, all but carved a slice off the gardener, who feelingly remarked to the footman that he had "never felt so like a cowcumber in all his life." The terrible weapon was then handed round for general inspection. All through the evening it had been, by a flight of fancy bordering on monomania, invested with a terrific attribute of sharpness, and now, while the females shuddered and shrank away from it, the males cautiously ran their thumbs along the edge and whistled expressively, as if words failed to do it justice. It was indeed a trusty blade, and one which, in the grasp of a skilled swordsman, might have severed an entire pat of butter at one blow.

CHAPTER IV.

Family presentations — True generosity — Great expectations—Noble sacrifice on the part of a relative—A virtuous and accomplished bird.

IN anticipation and preparation the days passed quickly away, and it was now nearly time for Verisopht to obey his country's call to duty. As the hour of separation drew near he became the recipient of many suitable gifts from a large circle of friends and relatives. Many of these presents were handsome and costly, but none of them awakened such heartfelt gratitude as the more simple and homely souvenirs from his brothers and sisters. Fanny worked for him a banner screen emblazoned with the family arms, "pieman rampant" and "son of a sea-cook hornpipant," and with the motto "Semper virens" worked in appropriately coloured silk; Carry made him a teapot cosy, a pair of slippers, and an antimacassar; Peter presented him with his translation, in his own handwriting, from Cæsar, neatly bound in brown paper; and the twins, who came next, pressed on his acceptance their little all, a small hutch containing a brace of guinea-pigs.

"Though I cannot see what possible use the guinea-pigs will be to Verisopht," reasoned Mr. Boomershine within himself, "still it is better to let the twins give what they prize most. Liberality with what is not theirs will come naturally enough; but liberality with what is will not be so easily acquired; and the quality, in its latter and purer form, cannot be encouraged too early. If I were to give them a couple of pounds to buy some little present for Verisopht, there would be no real generosity on their part. It would merely be a present from *me* through *them*. By all means then," observed Mr. Boomershine, as he buttoned up the two pounds in his pocket, and thought of the fruitful source of dirt and tears that would depart with the guinea-pigs—" by all means, then, let me foster this spirit of true generosity. The only worldly possessions to which the younger members of my family may be said to hold undisputed title consist mainly of live stock—rabbits, kittens, and silkworms; and I do think," argued Mr. Boomershine, as he recalled the oft-experienced sensation of treading on a fine fat silkworm, or sitting on a lively kitten, "this would be a favourable opportunity of implanting in their little bosoms the germs of true generosity—that is, giving away what is their own."

Luckily for Verisopht, the germs were not planted, for the "little bosoms," on the attempt being made, proved too hard and stony ground for the operation.

There was a great deal of surmise and conjecture throughout the whole family as to what "Aunt Millicent's" present would be. Aunt Millicent was Mrs. Boomershine's aunt, a Miss Simple. She was thus Verisopht's great-aunt. She was also his godmother. She was also a spinster. She was also rich. Altogether, then, it was expected that Aunt Millicent would come down handsome on the occasion. On this supposition, the carrier's cart, which passed at the bottom of the drive, was watched every evening with eager eyes. It never deposited, however, any precious burden, but either went on its way unheeding, or else merely stopped to deliver some lowly article of a household nature. This delay, instead of damping, on the contrary, inflamed the general expectation to such a pitch, that had a troop of white elephants, laden with precious stones, turned into the drive, the spectacle would have excited but little astonishment amongst the younger members of the family, who would at once have attributed it to Aunt Millicent's generosity.

At last, the very morning before Verisopht was to start, the postman brought a letter directed to him in the well-known stiff and minute handwriting of Aunt Millicent. The family were at breakfast, and they all watched Verisopht with breathless interest. Here was the present at last, or, at any rate, the herald of its approach!

Verisopht opened the envelope carefully, so as not to damage the cheque or banknote for a fabulous amount which, doubtless, lurked within. But neither cheque nor note was there.

" Read it out, Verry, my boy," said Mr. Boomershine, composing himself to listen.

Verry obeyed.

"' Dear Verisopht,

"' You are going to be a soldier. For my own part I would sooner you had been a tinker or a tailor, as those paths of life, if lowly, are yet comparatively free from the temptations which beset the one you have chosen. However, though not approving of your choice, I have the same affection for you as ever ; and so strong is my desire for your welfare, that the gift I am about to confer on you is one requiring a great sacrifice on my part——'"

"'Great sacrifice,'" thought Mr. Boomershine, " why, it must be an enormous sum !" and the tears of gratitude almost stood in his eye as he interpolated : " Aunt Millicent is a thorough Christian. Although I do not hold with her in her opinion concerning your profession, still I will say this of her, nothing can stifle her generosity. Proceed, Verry, my boy."

Verisopht himself was visibly affected as he continued :

"' Now, my dear Verry, I know you will value my present, not only for the sake of the donor, but also for the sake of the dear bird himself——'

" The *what ?*" asked the family, in one breath.

" The bird," faltered Verisopht.

" Proceed," said Mr. Boomershine, in a voice hollow and weak.

"' Yes, Verisopht, for your sake, I am about to part with what money would never have tempted, nor violence extorted, from me—my grey parrot, Mentor. And I will tell you why. He is no silly creature, perpetually inviting attention to his own beauty, or bidding maids in familiar terms to put the kettle on or take it off again. There is none of this foolish levity about him. It has been my pleasure for years to teach him a choice collection of moral precepts and admonitions; and amidst those temptations to which your future mode of life will expose you, in the vortex of vain frivolities, amidst the ribald jests and the ready oaths of a licentious soldiery, his peaceful utterances will fall on your ears with a sweet and purifying effect. You will receive him by a special messenger soon after you get this. My heart is too full to write more.

"'Your affectionate aunt,
"'MILLICENT SIMPLE.

"'P.S.—I have just parted from him. His last words were, "Be temperate in all things." He doubtlessly alluded to my grief. He is indeed a virtuous bird.

Take care of him. A lump of sugar and the enunciation of his name, " Mentor," in a soothing tone of voice will bring him to your finger. You might occasionally hang him up amongst the soldiers with beneficial results to them — poor benighted ones! Bless you!'"

In the course of the day Mentor arrived, and Verisopht, on introducing himself to " the virtuous bird" on the principles given in his aunt's postscript, found that he not only came to his finger with surprising alacrity, but also left a deep mark of his esteem upon it.

CHAPTER V.

Go where glory waits thee — A soldier's tear — Mentor improves the occasion with doubtful results—He indulges in a light repast and suffers therefrom—Gone away!—Outraged modesty—Mr. Boomershine renders himself liable to prosecution by the Society for the Protection of Women—Exciting scene—Painful separation.

E will not dwell on the parting between Verisopht and the family. He may or may not have shed a soldier's tear on the occasion; but that he *did* do so red-hot pincers will not extort from us. We will admit that for the first few miles of the railway journey up to Paddington the tip of his nose and his eyelids were red, but farther than that we will not go.

Mr. Boomershine accompanied him as far as London, with the intention of seeing him fairly started from Waterloo station; for Verisopht, even under the most favourable circumstances, had already evinced a surprising aptitude for getting into wrong trains, losing his ticket, and leaving his property behind him.

The heavy luggage had been forwarded to its destination by goods train; but notwithstanding this our hero's baggage formed a very imposing pile. Besides the usual portmanteaux and hat-boxes, there were dressing-bags, despatch-boxes, uniform-cases, and all these, together with Mentor in his cage, and the guinea-pigs in their hutch, constituted a very serious impediment to rapid locomotion. The consequence was that as the two cabs, chartered for the journey between Paddington and Waterloo, crawled in at one end of the latter station, Verisopht's train gracefully glided out at the other. This was the five o'clock train, and there was nothing for it but to wait until the one leaving at 8.30. Losing the train was provoking, but still there was one thing to be grateful for, and that was, it afforded Mr. Boomershine ample time to settle the claims of the cabmen without that injustice which might otherwise have been done them in the confusion of a hurried departure. The feelings of one of these hard-worked and virtuous men had been outraged by Mentor, who, from his position on the roof of the cab, had uttered certain temperance doctrines not in accordance with his views, and Mr. Boomershine would have been no tolerant Christian had he withheld the extra shilling demanded as compensation for wounded feelings. The other cabman, too, was a worthy fellow. He certainly did admit in homely language—rough, honest soul—that his " crock might 'a come along a bit farster, but the fact was he couldn't find it in 'is 'cart to 'it 'im," and, alas! the scant remuneration he received from an ungenerous public would not admit of his buying a better one. Base indeed that mortal who could have turned a deaf ear to this, and the appeal went straight to Mr. Boomershine's waistcoat pocket.

Nothing could now exceed the civility of the porters who had witnessed the whole transaction. Indeed they quite squabbled amongst themselves, simple-minded fellows, for the honour of carrying Mr. Boomershine's luggage, and crowded round with obsequious cap-touchings and civil cries of "Where to, sir?"

"Aldershot," replied Mr. Boomershine, with a pleasant sort of idea that they took him for a general, travelling down to the camp attended by his *aide-de-camp*.

The luggage was soon labelled and piled up to await the next train, and Mr. Boomershine enlisted the porters in the cause of its safe custody in much the same way as a recruit is enlisted in the service of his country. He was pleased to remark that there was no grasping avarice about these men, no ostentatious holding out of hands; but, on the contrary, each received his remuneration in an unobtrusive manner that made Mr. Boomershine quite regret that the station-master, who stood near, had not witnessed their delicacy of feeling.

The object was now to while away the next three hours, and, with this in view, Mr. Boomershine and Verisopht started off towards the Strand. It was an unfortunate hour. It was too late for those calm joys afforded by the Monument, the British Museum, and St. Paul's Cathedral; and too early for the theatres and other places of amusement; so the business on hand resolved itself into first doing the shop-windows in the Strand, and then having a quiet dinner at the Charing Cross Hotel.

When they had satisfactorily concluded this last act, they proceeded once more to Waterloo Station, and here they found a great many young men, all smoking, laughing, and talking, and walking up and down the platform, awaiting the departure of the train. There was a something about them that told Verisopht and his father they were young officers on their way down to Aldershot, and, amongst the others, they particularly noticed one who seemed on good terms with himself and every one else. There was no time, however, to be wasted, and they proceeded at once to look after the luggage. There it was, a goodly pile. But, consternation! where was Mentor?

"They sought him above; they sought him below;
They sought him with feelings of grief and of woe."

But, alas! they sought him in vain. The precious moments were waning fast, and still they searched without success. One porter solemnly averred that he had affixed a label to a bar of his cage, and had seen him "all right on the platform after the gents left the station." They were just giving up the search in despair, when a moral precept was heard to proceed from the Lost Property Office, and they found him holding forth to a congregation of lost articles. Having been found, it appeared, on the platform without a label, he had been taken there for safe custody. His label was gone, doubtless, and, as a portion of it was found sticking to his bill, the presumptive conclusion was that he had eaten it, paste and all, under the impression that it was edible, and placed there for his consumption.

They were just bearing the virtuous creature off in triumph, when a savage "W-whoop!" and a shriek of "Gone away!" attracted their attention to an excited mob of porters and passengers, headed by the volatile young officer they had already noticed, in hot pursuit of some animal. What was it? Heavens, a guinea-pig! With bitter thoughts of what the twins' feelings would have been, Verisopht and his father dashed down the platform to the rescue. Mr. Boomershine soon led the van, and so hotly pressed the guinea-pig that, in its indiscriminating terror, it took refuge in the voluminous folds of an old lady's dress, whither Mr. Boomershine, in the ardour of the chase, followed it. The old lady could only ejaculate, "Oh! Oh!! Oh!!!" each time in a louder key; but if there was a sameness in her remarks, she had a way of emphasising them with her umbrella which, though it at first seemed to make more impression on Mr. Boomershine's hat than his mind, eventually recalled that gentleman to a true sense of the proceedings. In vain did he then doff his battered hat, and hold out the recaptured guinea-pig as a living apology. The old lady was not to be appeased, but stood defiantly smoothing her ruffled plumes, and muttering, "Guinea-pig or no guinea-pig, she wasn't going to be insulted in public by the likes of him." The more abject Mr. Boomershine became in his apologies, the higher position of outraged modesty the old lady took up, until at last all further colloquy was cut short by the guard of the train shouting out, "Now then, take your seats, please!"

The engine screamed angrily; so did the old lady, that Mr. Boomershine would hear more from the Secretary of the Society for the Protection of Women; and the porters shouted, "Look sharp,

Drawn by R. Caldecott.]

"HE WOULD BE A SOLDIER!"

"Mr. Boomershine held out the recaptured guinea-pig as a living apology."

sir!" Verisopht was bundled into a compartment, and the guinea-pigs, with Mentor, into the guard's van. It was a moment of intense excitement.

"Good-bye! Bless you, my boy, bless you!" said Mr. Boomershine.

And so they parted—father and son; the son to be whirled off in a state of agonising perplexity; the father to be led away, perchance to durance vile, on a disgraceful charge of assaulting an unprotected female.

CHAPTER VI.

Is an important one—Our hero makes the acquaintance of a distinguished brother officer and at once profits thereby. He obtains a great deal of information of a novel character—He is guilty of wholesale traduction of character, and wounds one gentleman in his tenderest point—He engages in a transaction of a mysterious nature with a barmaid which gets him into a ticklish position, and finally results in an engagement—He arrives at Aldershot.

IT would be heartless to keep the reader in that state of suspense concerning Mr. Boomershine's fate which the conclusion of the last chapter has doubtless thrown him or her into. So, although our course lies properly with the anguish-stricken son *en route* for

Aldershot, we will linger for one moment on the platform, to present the father in the act of following his country's example, and settling the difficulty by paying his way out of it.

Unfortunately for Verisopht's peace of mind, he had been unable to witness this satisfactory *dénouement*, and for many miles of his journey he sat haunted by the spectacle of his father, as he had last beheld him, confronted by the enraged female. As the train drew up at Surbiton Station, the station-master shouted out to the guard :

"I say, Thompson, see if you've got a passenger of the name of Boomershine in a first-class smoking compartment."

"Any gent here o' the name o' Moonshine?" asked the guard, popping his head into the window.

"Yes, oh yes—at least my name is Boomershine. What is it?" asked Verisopht with a blushing and utterly groundless apprehension that the other passengers regarded him as a detected sharper.

"All right, sir; here you are," shouted out the guard to the station-master.

"V. S. R. S. Boomershine, Esquire?" asked the latter official, as his face appeared at the window in the place of the former's.

"Yes, that's me," said Verisopht with a palpitating heart.

"Here's a telegram for you, sir—sent down from the Superintendent's office at Waterloo."

"Oh, thank you."

What could have happened! The paternal mansion in flames and his relatives in cinders was the first picture that rose before his excited imagination.

With trembling hands he tore open the envelope and read the following telegram from his tender-hearted and thoughtful father:—

"WATERLOO STATION. 8.40 P.M.

"MY DEAR BOY,—I cannot bear the thought of your very first outset in life being clouded by anxiety. All is amicably arranged with that dreadful female, and I leave this station without a stain on my character. I shall return home this very night. They tell me here that this will catch you at Surbiton. In your letter home you need not allude to the unfortunate transaction. Let it be buried in the oblivion it merits. God bless you, my dear boy."

Such was the message of peace which, in the sender's fulness of heart, exhausted no less than three telegraph forms.

Owing to the dimness of the lamps or of Verisopht's own eyes—probably of both—he was a long time over the words, and for some weak moments he felt that manly independence and military renown would be as dust in the balance if weighed with the chance of returning to the quiet country home that night with his father. His sword in its leather case tumbling on his head from the rack above, here re-called him to himself, and these unworthy thoughts were banished.

By this time his perturbed feelings had

calmed down sufficiently to admit of his looking about him. He had been awakened out of his reverie by a violent fit of coughing, and he found that the compartment was full of smoke. He could hear a great deal of laughing and talking going on, but could see little of the speakers, who were enveloped in clouds of their own manufacture. He could count, however, that there were five of them, by the glowing ends of their cigars, which looked like gas-lamps in a London fog. At last, as his eyes became used to the atmosphere, he made out the volatile young gentleman who had headed the chase after the guinea-pig, sitting opposite to him. This young man seemed to enjoy no small share of popularity; and his remarks, which were nearly incessant, were received with great laughter and applause. He was evidently recounting some anecdote, but as the actors and the expressions used were unknown to Verisopht, he could merely take his cue when to laugh from the others, and this he did, in remembrance of his father's advice to adapt himself to different phases of society.

"I was doing galloper, you know, to old Squaretoes," said the young man, "and so I saw the whole thing. Well, the bugle sounded 'Commanding officers to the front,' and it was a caution to snakes to see the old Flapper come lolloping along on that rat-tailed gee of his, arms and legs all over the shop. 'Why didn't you bring that regiment of yours up by double column of companies?' roared old Squaretoes. 'Because you told me not to,' said the Flapper. '*I* told you not to! Did *I* tell him not to do so?' said Squaretoes, turning to Cocky Turnbull. 'Yeth you did, thir,' said Cocky—you know Cocky's way? By Jove! you should have heard old Squaretoes let fly. He nearly blew Cocky clean out of his saddle, eyeglass and all. It was a screaming good sell, though, wasn't it?"

This was received with shouts of laughter from every one except Verisopht, who was as much in the dark as if the narrator had been a Choctaw Indian conversing in his native tongue. Cocky! Flapper! gee! all over the shop! galloper! Would the proud day ever arrive when *he* should be able to converse in this strain? Would *he* ever be able to raise such shouts of laughter by a story of a flapper, a cocky, and a gee?

In such ambitious forecasts, Verisopht was too wrapt to join in the general merriment; but the narrator, mistaking his coughs and his streaming eyes—the result of the smoke—for unfeigned paroxysms of mirth, was pleased to offer him a cigar.

"No, I thank you," said Verisopht, very much flattered by the attention on the part of so great a personage. "I have never smoked, and, indeed, I should scarcely like to venture, for I have been told by my father that the first attempts are invariably attended with most unpleasant sensations."

This was Verisopht's opening speech, and, though deeply blushing the while, he delivered it with great pains, after the manner of Masters Sandford and Merton, whom he had always made his conversational models when on his best behaviour.

On this there were a great many winks, and whispers of "What a cure!" "Where was he riz, I wonder?" &c.

"Are you going to Aldershot?" asked the gentleman who had offered the cigar.

"Yes: I am going to join my regiment, in accordance with the instructions contained in—"

"Oh, yes, exactly. What regiment?"

"The 119th."

At this there were general cries of "Hulloa, Wilder, your fellows will learn a thing or two now!" "I say, Hooky, you'll be getting so precious sharp, you'll be cutting all your old friends," &c.

"The devil you are," said the gentleman addressed as "Hooky" and "Wilder." "Why, that's *my* regiment."

"Is it?" said Verisopht; "well, I *am* pleased to hear that. I am so glad to have met with one of my brother-officers. Is Aldershot a nice place?"

"Oh, delightful," replied Wilder. "One

of the most charming spots. Did you ever hear it called the Garden of England?"

"No, I don't know that I ever did," replied Verisopht.

"Well, neither have I; but that title would, without doubt, be conferred on it, were the beauties of the Long Valley more generally known."

"And what is the Long Valley?"

"Oh, it's where we go and pick primroses and lilies of the valley on Sunday afternoons."

"That's when they're in season, of course?" said Verisopht proudly, conscious of having been rather sharp.

"Of course; but when they're not, we botanise. Vegetation in that fertile spot is almost tropical in its growth, and offers a tempting field to the botanist."

Here there was much tittering, and a murmur ran through the compartment that "Hooky Wilder was in form to-night."

"Well now," said Verisopht enthusiastically, "I'd give a golden guinea if my aunt could hear all that. You won't be angry at what I'm going to say now?" he asked, looking round.

"No, no, not in the least," chorused every one.

"Well—well, she says— No, but really, I hardly—"

"Fire away!" "Go ahead!" proceeded from different occupants of the compartment.

"Well, she thinks officers dreadfully wild, and says they think nothing of getting— No, but really now, you know, are you sure you won't be offended?"

On this Wilder seized him by the hand, and pressed him to unburthen his bosom.

"Well, that you'd think nothing of getting just a little— No, but really, I hardly like—"

"Cut away!" said every one.

"Well, just a little—tipsy."

The word was hardly out of Verisopht's mouth before he bitterly repented his outspoken candour. There was a general burst of indignation. Some put their handkerchiefs up to their faces; some hid their burning countenances behind their newspapers; and one gentleman, who had been very drowsy all the time, on being now roused up to have the foul aspersion explained to him, said he had never been "sho 'shulted in all life," adding, as he dropped off to sleep again, "he'sh wounded me in tenderesht point." Poor Wilder was very much affected. He buried his face in his handkerchief, and his whole frame shook with the intensity of his emotion.

"Oh don't, please don't! Really I didn't mean—I didn't think—" stammered poor Verisopht.

"Well, promise us one thing," said Wilder, seizing his hand: "promise us, my young Christian friend—if you'll allow me to call you so—"

Verisopht could only reply by a pressure of the hand.

"Promise us that you will write to your aunt, and tell her how wickedly, how grossly, she has been deceived."

"I will," said Verisopht : " I promise you all I will."

"Thank you. It will take such a dreadful load off all our minds. And now let us dismiss this painful subject. We are now close to Woking station. I vote we go odd man out for a B. and S. all round."

The proposal was carried *nem. con.*, and Verisopht was initiated into the mysteries of "odd man out," and a "B. and S.," before he was many minutes older. He was a little surprised to find that "B. and S." was a beverage, of which one of the ingredients was an ardent spirit; and Wilder, reading this surprise in his expressive countenance, kindly explained the matter.

"You see, it having been brought to the notice of the Commander-in-Chief that the night air about Woking is injurious, owing probably to the vicinity of the cemetery, he has issued an order that all officers on passing through the station are to fortify themselves against the malaria. It is a great nuisance. But obedience is the first duty of a soldier, and, no matter what violence we do to our feelings, the order must be obeyed."

Verisopht was much obliged to Wilder for the kind explanation; and, fired by the noble example of cheerful obedience set him by his companions, he finished the liquid to the very last dregs; though, as he explained in a subsequent letter to his parents, it was the most nauseous draught he had ever tasted, and reminded him forcibly of coal-tar and soapsuds, besides imparting a balloon-like sensation to the drinker.

Before leaving Woking Verisopht was observed to linger behind and to engage in a transaction of a hurried and mysterious nature with the attendant damsel at the bar. Whatever it was, there was only just time to complete it and take his seat before the train moved off.

"Ah, you sly rascal!" said Wilder. "We saw you—after the petticoats, eh? I was just such another young dog in my day."

And here Wilder poked Verisopht in

the ribs, and made that peculiar noise which generally accompanies the action, and which is supposed to take up the sly insinuation at that point where words fail.

As Wilder's example was followed by all those who were near enough, and as Verisopht was both ticklish and shy, his repudiation of the soft impeachment was rather confused and incoherent.

"No, indeed!—Now really!—Oh, I say! —Well, I'm sure!—Oh, now you've spoilt them all!"

"Spoilt what?" asked Wilder.

"Why," replied Verisopht, holding something out of sight and looking round him pleasantly, "I thought it would be a capital treat, and a little return, you know, for all your kind explanations."

As he spoke he produced from behind him a paper bag containing twelve jam puffs, and with a pleasant consciousness of the fast nature of the proceeding, commenced by handing Wilder one.

"Well, you know," said Wilder, dubiously poising the tart on his forefinger, "we should be delighted; but, unfortunately, we are forbidden by the rules of the service to eat such things on pain of—well, not exactly death," said Hooky, placing his hands tenderly on his waistcoat, "it comes under the head of 'conduct unbecoming the character of an officer and a gentleman.'"

"You don't say so!" said Verisopht, with a blank expression of dismay, and the Simon blood curdled in his veins with horror.

"Yes; we take an oath on joining to eschew all such vanities as jam puffs, toffee, and hardbake. However, I know of nothing in the Queen's Regulations forbidding their external application, so here goes."

Suiting the action to the words, Wilder, amidst a shout of laughter, took such an unerring aim at the gentleman in the corner, who had been "sho 'shulted" by Aunt Millicent's opinion, and was now fast asleep again, that the jam puff split into numerous fragments on that feature immediately above the one where jam puffs usually complete their destiny.

" How curshed fliesh tchickle !" was all the remark the gentleman made, as he brushed away a few imaginary blue-bottles. Then hearing a good deal of laughter going on, he appeared to think that something convivial and cheery was expected from him, and at once broke out into a song suggested by the two predominant ideas on his mind at the moment—conviviality and flies :

" 'Passh bo'l whenumdgry,
Brush 'way blue-chaiied fly.' '

On a second application, however, he woke up to a foggy sense of affairs, and, seizing the fragments around him, returned the fire with such wildness that Verisopht's horrified countenance came in for a decoration of preserved fruit instead of Wilder's.

" What's in an aim ?" said Hooky, as he took another shot which showed that at all events there was a tolerable amount of accuracy in *his*, for again the missile hit its mark full and fair.

This was the signal for a general action. Verisopht's bag was seized, and the pastry flew about in clouds, while the raspberry-jam adhering to the countenances and clothes of the combatants, lent quite a sanguinary aspect to the affair.

At this strange scene Verisopht looked on aghast, thinking that all this was perhaps rather more unbecoming the characters of officers and gentlemen than if they had quietly eaten the tarts. But he kept his thoughts to himself, which, considering the reckless spirit now possessing his companions, was the best thing he could have done.

The engagement raged with considerable fury until all the ammunition was expended, and then after the storm came calm reflection. "Jam satis," said Wilder. The incoherent gentleman in the corner said it was "all rot," and resumed his slumbers; another gentleman who had enjoyed it all very much while it lasted now peevishly remarked, as he scraped the remains of a jam tart off his white waistcoat, that it was "All deuced fine, you know, but if ever you were in Hooky Wilder's company you were certain to find yourself let in for some infernal piece of madness;" and finally they all, with some returning sense of propriety, gathered up the telltale *débris* into Verisopht's hat-box.

After this our hero, slightly under the influence of the unaccustomed potation, became very talkative, and underwent the process of being drawn out, until his hearers knew all about Aunt Millicent and Mentor, the twins' guinea-pigs, his sisters' accomplishments, and Peter's proficiency in Latin. The confidences best received were those relating to Aunt Millicent and his sisters; and altogether the time passed pleasantly enough until the train drawing up amidst monotonous cries of "'Shot! 'Shot!" apprised them all that they had arrived at the station for that military hotbed, the Camp of Aldershot.

CHAPTER VII.

Introduction to military life--A pleasant *jeu d'esprit*, entitled "The Sleeper Awakened" — Striking ceremony of initiation—Sub-Lieutenant Boomershine lies like a warrior taking his rest, and doesn't much like it.

THERE were several soldiers standing about on the platform, and Verisopht, noticing that each wore a band round his arm with the letters M.P on it, asked Wilder what it meant.

"It is a badge of infamy," was the reply. "They are men who have got drunk four times within a year, and in such detestation is this crime held by the British soldier, that when one of them commits himself to this extent he is looked upon as something to be wondered at, and is labelled, as you perceive, 'Miraculous Phenomenon.' Just see how they gather round that man as if welcoming him into the degraded brotherhood;" and as Wilder spoke, the "Miraculous Phenomenons" swooped down upon a soldier in a very advanced stage of intoxication, who had just tumbled out of a third-class carriage, and bore him away, their burden all the time applying to a public body he called the "mil'ry pleesh," certain expressions which Verisopht, until Wilder enlightened him, had not the slightest idea were terms of endearment. Indeed, from the tones in which they were couched, he should have supposed they had been quite the reverse. What a lesson was here afforded him not to judge by first appearances; and being an affectionate lad, he committed a few of the endearing epithets to memory, with the intention of applying them to his father when next they met. He also took a mental note of the whole scene as an interesting item in his first letter to Aunt Millicent, and congratulated himself upon having found a cicerone like Wilder, who seemed to know everything, and never to be at a loss for an explanation.

The members of the party, belonging to different regiments, now separated and went their several ways, but not before they had bid Verisopht an affectionate farewell, and requested that they might be remembered in the kindest terms to his aunt when he next wrote to her.

"Now," said Verisopht to Wilder, "I call that being really pleasant and friendly. I do wish my aunt could only have heard them. I am sure she would have been gratified beyond measure. Do you know she says——"

"Never mind your aunt for the present," said Wilder, who was a man of action, and had taken Verisopht under his wing—a wing, be it remarked, apparently addicted to daring flights of fancy. "Let's get your traps together, and get away up to barracks.

It will be too late to arrange anything tonight, and I'll give you a shake-down in my quarters. You don't mind roughing it, I suppose?"

Verisopht explained that he positively thirsted for hardships, and as he did so, he almost felt that nothing short of a bullet in the brain would slake his thirst for glory. At all events, it would have stopped his asking for more.

"'He jests at scars that never felt a wound,'" said Wilder. "Wait a bit, until you have had a little taste of it; or if you find it impossible to restrain your ardour, you can commence at once by sitting down all to-night in my tub, with the hose of the barrack engine directed down your back, and worked by a fatigue party. It will give you a capital idea of the Autumn Manœuvres at Dartmoor, and you'll be doing quite as much good to yourself and your country."

The remembrance of his mother's parting injunctions on the subject of guarding against colds and coughs restrained Verisopht from closing with this kind offer, and he confusedly murmured his intention of waiting until hardships came in his way, and then taking them coolly.

"That's right: now come along," and Wilder, for whom the porters bustled about with smiling alacrity as if he were a well-known character, soon had everything ready for a start.

The luggage was piled up on the roof of the fly, and surmounting the whole was Mentor, while the guinea-pigs, as befitted their inferior attainments, occupied a less exalted position underneath the cage of that accomplished animal. The virtuous bird was evidently far from well. He was probably suffering from label on the chest; but whether it was the paper, the paste, or the print that had disagreed with him, it is impossible to say. Finding himself, however, in this commanding position, and apparently thinking that something was expected from him, he summoned up enough energy to croak out in sepulchral tones, "Evil communications corrupt good manners," a statement much relished by the bystanders.

"M Lines, North Camp," shouted Wilder to the driver of the fly, and the vehicle moved off at a majestic rate amidst the applause of a knot of porters, at whom Mentor had let off a parting precept. Thus fired to the performance of still nobler deeds, the virtuous creature then addressed himself, through the bottom of his cage, to the regeneration of the guinea-pigs.

As they drove on, Verisopht looked eagerly out of the windows for those military sights which he expected would burst upon his gaze at every moment; but he was disappointed to find that the town of Aldershot, as well as he could see by the gaslight, had nothing distinctively military about it, with the exception of a red-coat here and there, and was very much like any other English town. When they emerged from the streets, however, his martial soul was gladdened by the sight of immense blocks of brick buildings, gleaming with lights, and teeming with military life.

There were bugles and trumpets sounding, fifes and drums playing tattoo at one end of a square, a regimental band playing outside the officers' mess at the other, non-commissioned officers calling over the rolls at the top of their voices, and men shouting back in response. Altogether, Verisopht thought it one of the most inspiriting scenes he had ever witnessed. These were the permanent barracks, as Wilder informed him, and, after leaving them, they passed through an interminable succession of rows of low black, wooden huts; and here again, in different parts, there were more bugles, and bands, and hoarse roll-calls. At last, after a great deal of shouting from Wilder, the fly drew up at one of the huts, which Wilder informed Verisopht was "his diggings."

With the assistance of Wilder's servant, who was on the look-out, the luggage was soon transferred to one of the small rooms and the passage of the establishment; after which, Wilder and Verisopht betook themselves to the anteroom of the mess.

Verisopht was rather nervous and shy as he approached the red-curtained hut, and he pictured to himself a gay host of red-coated gentlemen jumping up to welcome their newly-joined brother in arms, perhaps with some peculiar ceremony, perhaps with outspoken *bonhomie*, certainly with courtesy.

As he entered, his eyes wandered round the room for what he had expected, and he found that his imagination had carried him rather wide of the mark. There was not a soul to be seen at first, and it was only when a deep snore, proceeding from the depths of an arm-chair, caused him to look in the direction whence it came, that he saw two legs, with a red stripe down each, protruding from under a newspaper; from which he gathered that the owner of the military legs had fallen asleep while reading the news.

Hooky Wilder held up his finger in mute appeal to Verisopht to be silent, and noiselessly stepped across the room on tiptoe.

"How considerate," thought Verisopht.

"He is doubtless anxious not to disturb the poor fellow, worn out with his arduous duties."

The considerate Wilder's movements now became very mysterious. He lighted a spill and carefully balanced it on the instep of the sleeper's patent-leather boot, at the same time explaining in a whisper to Verisopht that the heat would cause the leather to draw, and afford the sleeper the most delicious sensations of having a nice comfortable thumbscrew applied to his foot; and was, in short, one of the most pleasant methods of awakening any one. "In fact," concluded Wilder, "it is a pleasant little *jeu d'esprit*, entitled 'The Sleeper Awakened.'"

On this Verisopht became so interested in the process, with a view to hereafter practising it on his father, that he stooped low to watch the progress of the flame, and became so wrapped in his observations as not to notice that Wilder had slipped behind the sleeper's chair.

In the space of about five seconds there

was a violent upheaval of the newspaper, and the young seeker after practical knowledge, with a yell of mingled pain and wrath ringing in his ears, found himself taking an unexpected part in the one-act drama entitled "The Sleeper Awakened." It was not a pleasant nor a dignified part by any means, and merely consisted in being sharply smitten over the head with Hart's "Annual Army List," the nearest weapon that came to the awakened sleeper's hand. That highly respectable mixture, the commingled blood of the Simples, the Verisophts, the Raws, and the Boomershines boiled.

"Just you do that again!" said Verisopht.

His request was immediately complied with, and this time the action was accompanied by the angry queries, "Who the devil are you, sir? What the devil do you mean by—oh, you scoundrel, Hooky! it's you, is it?" And the speaker having been apprised of Wilder's presence by a stifled burst of laughter behind the chair, here spoke the soft word which turned away Verisopht's wrath just before it took the dangerous form of retaliation.

"I beg you ten thousand pardons," he said; "but you must admit that appearances were greatly against you, and I really thought that, in a total stranger, such a liberty amounted to downright impertinence."

Verisopht at once saw that there was reason in the other's words, and readily shook the hand held out to him.

"He is the new wart," said Wilder, by way of introduction.

"Oh, indeed!" said the young officer, and he again shook hands with Verisopht, this time in his capacity as the "new wart."

How differently to the ideal the real was gradually turning out. There was no martial welcome to the young aspirant to military renown; no peculiar ceremony of initiation; but here he was, first banged on the head with a book, and then introduced as a "wart."

"I don't wish to hurt your feelings, Boomershine," said Wilder, "but the fact is, 'wart' is a generic term for all sub-lieutenants. You see—and here again, pray excuse me—their position is lowly, and as the Duke of Wellington, or the Archbishop of Canterbury, or the beadle of Burlington Arcade, or some other high personage, remarked, they are mere excrescences on the face of society, and, as brevity is the soul of wit, the whole definition is summed up in the unpretending title of 'wart.'"

"Oh, indeed," said Verisopht, and he took a seat, and a mental note that he would not enter into this subject in his next letter home.

"Where are all the fellows to-night, Buffer?" asked Wilder.

"Oh, the regiment is dining with the Rifles," was the reply, "and there were only three of us at mess. Old Calipash has gone off awfully huffed because I wouldn't listen to his West Indian yarns; Slowcock has gone to his room to read for the Staff College; and I was on duty, worse luck to it."

"Who's in orders for duty to-morrow?" asked Wilder.

"You are," replied the other, with a chuckle.

"How's that? Where's Smiler?" indignantly asked Hooky. "He's next on the roster."

"Smiler got a telegram this morning saying his aunt's awfully bad, and he's off to the North."

"Come, I say," said Wilder in an injured tone of voice, "that's rather too much of a good thing. That's coming it rather too strong, upon my soul it is. That blessed old aunt of Smiler's is worth two months' leave in the year to him, and she always gets these sudden attacks just before his turn of duty. She's a gross imposition, and if he doesn't kill or cure her this journey I'll denounce her to the chief as the most gigantic fraud of the day. Anything been going on while I have been away?"

"Oh no, only the usual grind—field-day,

guard, court-martial; court-martial, guard, field-day. What sort of a time have you been having up in town?"

On this Wilder entered upon a very detailed and spirited account of his doings, and became so enigmatical that Verisopht, after trying for a long time to look as if he understood the many jokes with which the narrative was interspersed, at last sank into a slumber.

He must have dozed for about an hour when Wilder woke him up.

"Come along, Boomershine, you are tired; so am I; we'll turn in. I haven't had more than about five hours altogether between the sheets the whole three days I've been away, and, confound that aunt of Smiler's! I shall have to get up at six o'clock to-morrow. Buffer has gone to turn out the regimental guard."

Piloted by Wilder along the row of huts, which were bewilderingly alike, Verisopht soon found himself in the narrow, dark little passage which pierced the centre of Wilder's row.

"Here, take hold of the tail of my coat until I strike a light," said Wilder, as Verisopht attempted to force his way through one or two partitions, and perversely tried to walk up the one step that went down, and to walk down the one step that went up.

The kind offer was accepted in time to avert any serious catastrophe, and in a few moments a light shed its cheery rays on the scene.

Verisopht now found himself on the threshold of an Aldershot quarter. In point of size it was something between the Albert Hall and a pepper-caster. It could not boast of the proportions of the former, while at the same time it somewhat exceeded those of the latter. If a stranger, you nearly brained yourself when you entered, then you tumbled into the fireplace opposite before you knew you had got into the room, and in trying to recover yourself you all but went sideways through the window, and, finally, in your frantic efforts to avoid defenestration—an act you were at all events pretty sure to accomplish as far as your elbow-joint—you in all likelihood fell upon your host and knocked him down on his own hearth.

Occupying a considerable portion of the microscopic apartment was the bed which Wilder's servant had put up for Verisopht's reception.

"I hope you'll sleep comfortably," said Wilder; "it's only a camp-bed I had in the last autumn manœuvres; but it's a capital contrivance, and the best of it is it shuts up and goes into such a small space."

Verisopht wished his kind host goodnight; and not long after retiring to rest became practically acquainted with the advantages of a bed which "shuts up and goes into a small space." As he did not like to disturb Wilder and was utterly ignorant of the mechanism of the contrivance, he passed his first night as one of his country's defenders, rather more like a hedgehog than a soldier.

CHAPTER VIII.

First awakenings—A matinée militaire—Precept upon precept.

NOTWITHSTANDING the fatiguing and exciting incidents of the day, Verisopht passed a sleepless night. In addition to the discomfort of his position, he felt very strange, and, if the truth must be told, just a little home-sick.

The grey dawn was just struggling through the tiny little window, which matched the tiny little room, and he had just sunk off into slumber, when a clatter and din, re-echoing between the long rows of wooden huts, awakened him with a start.

It was the drums and fifes playing the *reveillée,* and, somehow, as he lay awake listening, the music in the early morn had rather a depressing effect. The tune—the one always played on the occasion, why or wherefore we know not—was that identical air to which he in his childhood had, and the twins in theirs still, sung certain words concerning an irreligious old Daddy Long-legs who wouldn't say his prayers. As the familiar ditty carried him back to his childish days in the quiet country home, there arose in Verisopht's heart a dull, aching thought that perhaps, notwithstanding all the youthful longings for man's estate, those days, now gone for ever, would be far away the happiest in his life. But this was a weakness soon conquered.

The noise did not seem to have much effect upon Wilder, for when it ceased Verisopht could hear him in the next room still snoring with unbroken regularity. The hum of barrack life now commenced in earnest, and sleep to a novice was out of the question. Bugling and trumpeting seemed to be going on in all directions; and to add to it all, Verisopht's tender heart was much wrung by what he took for the shrieks of a pig in its death-agony, which proceeded from the next lines, occupied by a Highland regiment. Then presently there was a great deal of stamping and tramping about outside, mingled with shouts of strange import. Voices, pitched in all keys, were hard at it:—" 'Old up yer 'eds!"—" Now then, don't lose that ther touch below the elber!"—" Cut away them 'ands more smarter!"—" Take his name down!"—" Right wheel!"—" At the last sound of the warrud, step off with the left fut!"—" Carry back them butts!" were some of the mysterious utterances which awakened his curiosity and wonder; while, through it all, one voice, which was fascinating in its monotony, kept up a continuous refrain of " One, tow—one, tow!"

Verisopht's eyes were not the only pair in the room wide awake and wonderingly staring. Mentor, too, had been aroused by the unaccustomed sounds, and for a long

time had been putting his head first on one side, then on the other, in vain attempts to take it all in, until, at last, as if put on his mettle, he sharpened up his bill on the wires of his cage and croaked out his entire string of moral precepts. This produced rather a confused jumble in Verisopht's head of—
"Now then, cut away them evil communications! one, tow—one, tow! Corrupt them 'ands more smarter! one, tow—one, tow! At the last sound of the warrud carry back them good manners! one, tow—one, tow," &c.

After some time of this confused medley, a knock resounded on the panels of the door, and a gruff voice said:

"Rations is ready, sir."

A snore was the only reply from Wilder.

"Rations is ready, sir, and they're a-waitin' for the orficer," again said the voice.

The snoring abated somewhat, and the voice, seizing the opportunity, came in again with—"The rations is ready, sir, and——"

"Go to the devil!" proceeded in sleepy tones from Wilder's pillow.

The man outside on this immediately betook himself down the passage, as if in prompt obedience to the mandate; then hesitated, as if uncertain at the moment how to carry it out; and, finally, he returned, and tried the announcement the other way.

"They're a-waitin' for the orficer, sir, and the rations is ready."

"Who's that?" said Wilder, at last aroused.

"The orderly corporal, sir. The rations is ready."

"Why the devil didn't you say so before? All right. Tell them to go on; I'll be out presently."

On this the orderly corporal retired, and Verisopht heard Hooky Wilder getting into his uniform to a running accompaniment of anathemas on Smiler's aunt's head.

Verisopht coughed.

"Holloa, Boomershine! how did you sleep?"

"Oh, very comfortably indeed, thank

you," replied Verisopht, who at the moment was feeling his back to see if he had contracted curvature of the spine for life.

"That's right."

And Wilder once more returned to "Smiler's aunt."

It was wonderful how quickly he slipped into his uniform, and, after waiting just a few moments to have a laugh at Verisopht's bed and to put it to rights, he buckled on his sword and clattered out of the hut.

His exit was speedily followed by the entrance of a closely-shorn and upright individual, who explained that he was Mr. Wilder's servant. He was dressed in well-cut but seedy *mufti*, and obviously caught his master's falling mantles.

"My master says I'm to do for you until you get a servant of your own, sir."

Verisopht, albeit there was rather a bloodthirsty sound about the announcement that he was to be done for, expressed himself greatly obliged.

"Mr. Wilder, he'll have his tub after

he's been round the men's breakfasts. Will you have yours now, sir, or wait till after?"

Verisopht thought he'd wait till after.

The man now asked for the keys of Verisopht's portmanteau and uniform-case, and proceeded to lay out the necessary articles for his temporary master's toilet.

During this operation Verisopht Boomershine was guilty of a piece of deception not at all in keeping with his usual honesty and candour. To all appearance he was sound asleep, but his deep blushes when the man took his brand-new razors out of their case, and laid them out for use, showed how wide awake he had been all the time, and how keenly alive he was to the hollow mockery of this last proceeding.

After this the man withdrew, to the unspeakable relief of Verisopht, who now fell into a real sleep, and slumbered on until aroused by the same individual.

"Mr. Wilder has gone to the mess for his breakfast, sir, and left word that you was to be woke up at nine, for the commanding officer will be at the orderly-room at ten, and you'll have to report yourself there to him. He said as soon as you was dressed you was to go to the mess for breakfast, sir."

With the dreadful possibility of keeping the Colonel waiting before his eyes, Verisopht quickly performed his ablutions, and donned with all expedition the uniform which had been laid out for him. He then started for the mess.

CHAPTER IX.

A trying ordeal—Curious phenomenon—The terrors of Martial Law.

IT was a very trying ordeal, making his way to the mess all by himself and in uniform. *En route* he met several soldiers, who, to his great discomposure, saluted. He did not know what was the correct thing to do in return. He did not think he ought to bow, and he did not think he ought to nod, so he compromised the matter with a sort of spiral twist from his waist upwards. This was in individual cases, but once when four men, sitting on a form, sprang up with one accord as he passed, and saluted like one man, he was so impressed by the collective compliment that he took off his cap and made a low bow. Without committing himself any further, however, he managed to reach the mess, and he entered amidst a great deal of laughter, above which he thought he heard Wilder's voice saying something about a parrot and guinea-pigs.

The mess-room was a long, low apartment, made as comfortable as a hut could be by means of carpets, curtains, and plate-covered side-boards. Down the centre ran a long table, laid for breakfast, at which numerous young men in uniform were sitting, some eating heartily, some reading the paper propped up against their coffee-pots as they toyed with the comestibles, while some were standing about and entering into the general conversation. As Verisopht's entrance was observed the laughter suddenly ceased, and Wilder took upon himself the duty of introduction, with "Gentlemen, allow me to introduce Mr. Boomershine."

Some of the men shook hands good-naturedly, and others who were farther away nodded cheerily, but one or two of the very youngest stared patronisingly.

"What'll you have for breakfast?" asked Wilder. "I didn't order it for you, as I didn't know what you'd like. Try a grilled dodo."

"Thank you, yes; you're very kind; I should like one very much, thank you," replied Verisopht, who did not exactly know whether he was standing on his head or on his heels.

"Here, waiter!"

"Yessir," replied a new waiter, who, being a recent importation from the ranks, and very new to the business, was carried away by over-anxiety to please.

"Order a dodo for Mr. Boomershine. Anything else, Boomershine?—a couple of eggs?"

"Thank you, yes," said Verisopht.

"Yessir," said the anxious waiter, and he rushed off with wonderful alacrity to an adjacent pantry, whence he was heard shouting out to the cook, "Two biled eggs and a dodo, and look sharp about that there dodo."

"Here, take a seat, Boomershine, and you can fire away at some of my tea and toast until your breakfast comes," said Wilder. "The chief goes to the orderly-room at ten, sharp; and if you're not there he'll go down your throat, spurs and all."

"Oh, please, sir," said the over-anxious waiter, re-entering, "the mess-man says he ain't got no dodos this morning."

"That's really unpardonable in him," remarked Wilder. "However, it can't be helped. Try a stewed peacock, Boomershine."

"Thank you. I think, perhaps, as there's not much time, I had better have some of this cold pie," said Verisopht, to whom the prospect of the Colonel "going down his throat, spurs and all," was a very terrible one indeed.

"What sort of a night had you at the

Rifles, Fluffy?" asked Wilder, as Verisopht took his seat at the table.

"Oh, precious wet."

"Well, it wasn't a particularly wet one here, was it, Boomershine?"

"No, indeed," replied Verisopht. "It is one of the most wonderful instances of partial rain I have ever heard of in all my life. It was quite starlight here."

"This is indeed refreshing," remarked old Captain Chutney, who had recently exchanged from India; and, as he held a tumbler in his hand, Verisopht thought he understood the allusion, and innocently joined in a general laugh.

There was a great deal of talking going on, and Verisopht, who did all the listening, was surprised at not being able to catch any of the officers' names with which he and his sisters had made themselves familiar by means of the Army List. In fact, Carry and Fanny had settled, to their own satisfaction, the personal appearance and dispositions of nearly every officer in the regiment. "Captain Mortimer," they had been quite sure, "was tall, with black, wavy hair, and dark, poetical eyes. Herbert Netherton was sad and pensive-looking, very poor, and passionately devoted to his mother, whom he supported out of his daily five and threepence. The Hon. Algernon Cecil Fitzroy was rather wild, but with lovely blue eyes and dark lashes. John James Smith was sandy-haired and freckled. Donald MacDonald MacStiggins had very red hair and high cheek-bones. Reginald Carrington Wilder" (the "Hooky" did not appear in the Army List) "was shy and retiring, and deeply studious;" and so on.

In vain Verisopht listened for Mortimer, or Fitzroy, or Smith, or Netherton. They were all Fluffies, or Podgies, or Buffers, or Hookies; in short, they all seemed to be called by any names but their proper ones, and he was unable to judge how far his sisters' surmises had been correct.

He was just beginning to get on good terms with a game-pie when a bugle sounded under the mess windows with an effect that was magical. Tea and buttered toast and plates were pushed away, caps were rammed on, and every one rushed out of the room.

"That's 'Prisoner's Call.' Come along, Boomershine, the chief's in the orderly-room."

Verisopht needed no second bidding, and, following the current, soon found himself in the orderly-room (a place where all the official business of a regiment is conducted), confronting an awful-looking personage who sat at a table in the centre of the room. He was very fussy and red —so much the latter that the facings of his coat seemed to be principally useful in showing where the cloth ended and the skin began. This was Colonel Rooteen, commanding the 119th Regiment.

"This is Mr. Boomershine, sir—come to join," said the adjutant, Lieutenant Dressop.

"Hum—ha. Come to join, eh? How d'ye do?" said Colonel Rooteen.

"Thank you, sir; I am quite——"

"Stay. You had better embody your

reply in the form of an official, and send it on through the proper channel to———"

"I don't think, sir, there is any occasion," said the adjutant.

"Never mind, Mr. Boomershine; sit down there, and I'll talk to you presently; and I *do* wish, Mr. Dressop, you would try and perfect yourself in your duties. Bring in the prisoners, sergeant-major."

Verisopht sat down on the extreme edge of a form, and observed further proceedings with eyes and mouth wide open.

"Shun! Ick—mow! How! Fr-r-ut! Scort—steese!" said the sergeant-major, in a sharp succession of barks, the result being that two men, one in full dress and with a drawn bayonet in his hand, the other in a shell-jacket and bare-headed, marched into the room at the bark "Ick—mow," stopped short at the bark "How," turned to their front, that is, faced the Colonel, at the bark "Fr-r-rut," and finally, at the concluding howl "Scort—steese," the escort, consisting of the man with the drawn bayonet, suddenly assumed a constrained position, which Verisopht afterwards learned was called "standing at ease."

All this was highly interesting, and there was a certain amount of awe on Verisopht's countenance as he found himself face to face with a malefactor of so deep a dye as to necessitate the presence of a guard with a drawn bayonet. This precaution was in itself a sufficient indication of the criminal's desperate character to prepare Verisopht for something very terrible.

"Read out the crime, Mr. Dressop," said the Colonel to the adjutant.

Verisopht hung on the adjutant's words.

"For refusing to wash his face when repeatedly ordered to do so by the orderly-sergeant of his company," read out the adjutant from a paper before him.

In vain the criminal attempted to excuse himself: his guilt was marked in every line of his countenance, and he was convicted and sentenced to condign punishment on the spot.

Again the sergeant-major barked mysteriously, and another desperado was brought in and charged.

"For saying, when ordered by Corporal Stickler to have his hair cut, 'Why, it was cut last Toosday; I'll be like a blessed kangaroo,' or words to that effect."

Equally in vain with the former criminal did this hardened reprobate endeavour to elude the grasp of martial law, and to him was meted out the full measure of retribution.

The connection between cropped heads and kangaroos did not transpire during the investigation, and at last Verisopht, with the thirst for knowledge strong upon him, whispered to Wilder:

"Why is a man with short hair like a kangaroo?"

"Come, come, sir!" said the Colonel sharply; "none of this unbecoming levity. This is neither the time nor place for asking riddles."

Verisopht was too confused to explain that the question had been put in no conundrummic spirit, and the business of "telling off prisoners" proceeded.

The spectacle which now followed was,

perhaps, a more painful one than was afforded by either of the preceding cases. Three young soldiers—indeed they were little more than boys—were brought in, all charged with the same crime.

"How young, and yet how depraved," thought Verisopht, as he gazed on their beardless faces. They were evidently fresh from the ennobling influences of their lowly but virtuous homes in the agricultural districts, and yet, alas! how soon had they fallen away from those lessons of probity and rectitude there taught them!

The Adjutant cleared his throat and read out:

"For conduct subversive of good order and military discipline in having, in the main street of Aldershot, on the afternoon of the 20th instant, squeaked derisively when passing Lance-Corporal Falsetto."

An episode connected with the defence afforded Verisopht some idea of the terrors of martial law. A young recruit, called by the accused to bear witness in their favour, solemnly averred that he was "passin' along at the time, and didn't 'ear no squeakin' nor nothink."

"Now, sir," said Colonel Rooteen severely, "do you know what will become of you if you tell a lie?"

"Yes, sir, go to ——, sir," replied the recruit.

"No, sir! by gad! much worse than *that*; you'll be tried by general court-martial," said Colonel Rooteen, blowing out his cheeks and rolling his eyes, until the recruit trembled from the ball tuft in his shako down to the nethermost nail in his ammunition boots.

Verisopht's heart sickened within him at the contemplation of all this wickedness, and he hardly knew what punishment overtook the delinquents.

This sort of work went on for some time, but at last these harrowing instances of human depravity came to a conclusion, and the Colonel once more turned his attention to Verisopht.

"Now, Mr. Dressop, post that young gentleman to a company at once, and take him out forthwith to drill. He wants setting up sadly."

Assuredly poor Verisopht did not want setting down, and his demeanour verged on the abject as he bowed to the Colonel and followed the adjutant out of the room.

"You see," said the Adjutant to Verisopht, as they walked to the barrack square, "the Colonel isn't in a very good temper to-day. The fact is we've been fighting the War Office for two years and a half over elevenpence threefarthings, and we've had rather bad news this morning. I'm afraid it will go against us;" and here the Adjutant shook his head sadly. "But"—and here the Adjutant ground his teeth savagely— "we'll fight it out to the bitter end."

By this time they had reached the square. Here the same monotonous hum of "One-tow—one-tow," "Take his name down," "Cut away them 'ands," was going on in all directions, while numerous batches of recruits were going through all sorts of extraordinary evolutions and contortions in obedience to these words of strange import.

"Corporal Stickler!" shouted out the adjutant to a non-commissioned officer who was doing the "one-tow" part of the business. In one moment the corporal was in front of the Adjutant, heels closed together, body rigid, and right hand up at the salute. He was a—but Drill Corporal Stickler deserves a new chapter.

CHAPTER X.

A terrible martinet—The correct position of a soldier—Touching instance of self-sacrifice on the part of Lieutenant Wilder—Our hero embarrasses himself with a gaunt giant in a shell-jacket—He falls into the hands of an Indian warrior and *Raconteur* of distinction—He makes a tour of inspection—The piping times of peace.

HE was a most fierce and warlike-looking individual, was Corporal Stickler. Alongside Corporal Stickler, Mars himself would have looked like a Methodist parson. His very boots, where they swelled over the corns and bunions, had a grape-shot-like appearance, and his very trousers, where they bagged and wrinkled at the knees, seemed to wear a settled frown on their surfaces. His nose was in keeping with his general fierce aspect, and was always highly inflamed. But his most aggressive feature was his moustache, which was of a fierce reddish tinge, and stuck straight out over his mouth like *chevaux-de-frise*. It was also suggestive of "fixed bayonets;" and an ardent kiss from Corporal Stickler—if he ever indulged in such a freak of nature—must have communicated to the fair one a sharp sensation of being cupped. Of all his terrors this last was, perhaps, the most dreaded; for when asking a recruit, with bitter irony, why he had not "cut away his 'and more smarter," or "stepped off with the left fut," he had a way of bringing his irate countenance so near his victim's face that the *chevaux-de-frise* wandered titillatingly about the wretched recruit's face, and woe to him if he lifted a hand to scratch or rub. In conclusion, Corporal Stickler's forage-cap was so much on the side of his head, that it appeared to be setting all laws of gravitation at defiance.

To the care of this worthy the adjutant handed over Verisopht.

Our hero's military career can hardly be said to have commenced until his introduction to Drill Corporal Stickler, for it was not till then that he had even the faintest idea of standing in the correct position of a soldier. On this point Corporal Stickler lost no time, and, handing over the charge of his batch of recruits to a subordinate, he devoted himself entirely to this important part of Verisopht's military education.

"Look at me, sir," said Corporal Stickler, "and stand as I do." And here Corporal Stickler figuratively swallowed a poker, and Verisopht feebly tried to do likewise.

"No, sir, that won't do, I'm afraid," said Corporal Stickler; and with a pitying smile he laid gentle but corrective hands on his pupil.

Under this manipulation Verisopht's heels were now closed together, his toes turned out, his shoulders drawn back, his elbows pressed close to his side, the palms of his hands turned to the front, his chest tapped, his chin raised, and finally, after thus trussing him, Corporal Stickler stepped back several paces to view his handiwork.

"Chest more out, sir. That ain't yer chest—that ain't yer chest, sir."

"Oh, I beg your pardon, I'm sure!" said Verisopht, blushing deeply, and hurriedly altering his position.

"Now, sir, that's as bad t'other way. You mustn't stand, sir, as if you was makin' a bow to the ladies."

"Dear me, it's really very hard. I had no idea it was such a hard thing to stand up straight," said Verisopht, as Corporal Stickler again laid hands upon him.

It was indeed very hard. If he tried to throw out his chest, he was tapped lower down and told to keep *that* in, and when he tried to do so, he was admonished on another point. It was very hard, too, to keep his hands turned out and his elbows close in; for when he turned out his palms his elbows came out too, and when he closed his elbows, his palms turned in

Altogether, it was so difficult a thing to do that the whole of his first drill was devoted to this one point.

As he was returning from his lesson he met Wilder, who asked him, with an anxious and serious air, if he had been measured for his sentry-box yet.

"No. Dear me, do you really mean to say——."

"'Do I really mean to say!' My dear fellow, how do you suppose you can learn the duties of a sentry without a sentry-box?"

Verisopht admitted that that would be impossible, and begged that Wilder would at once kindly afford him the benefit of his experience in repairing this or any other oversight.

"Very well," said Wilder, "I'll put you up to it all. You see you're posted to my company, and as the Captain is away on the staff, I'm expected to look after you. You had better come now and see me pay the men, and if you like I'll always let you do it yourself for the future."

Verisopht was exceedingly gratified at this mark of Wilder's confidence, and while accompanying him to the barrack-rooms expressed his gratitude in the warmest terms.

"Don't mention it, I beg," said Wilder; "I'd do a great deal more for you than that; and as the rooms have to be inspected every day by an officer of the company, I'll waive all claim to this privilege in your favour."

"But are you sure I'm not depriving you——"

"My dear Boomershine, what a life this would be were we not prepared to make occasional sacrifices for each other! Besides, I never can forget the kindness with which my seniors always gave up these little pleasures to me. I'll take no refusal, my dear Boomershine; you shall go round the room and pay the company every day."

Verisopht was deeply touched, and their arrival in the barrack-room alone cut short those words of gratitude with which his heart was full.

"Now, Sergeant Tout, Mr. Boomershine is posted to this company and will want a servant. What man do you recommend?" asked Wilder, as soon as he had initiated his subaltern into the method of paying a company.

"There's Jukes, sir; he's a handy sort of a man."

"Isn't big enough. You see," explained Wilder to Verisopht. "I'd advise you to have a big man, for then he can't wear your clothes."

Verisopht assented to this, and on this principle of selection he soon found himself the embarrassed master of a gaunt giant in a shell jacket.

This man was a fearful weight on Verisopht's mind. There was no work to give him, and wherever he went that morning the gaunt giant followed. There was no escape from him. He blockaded the doors of the ante-room and the mess-room, and when Verisopht was in one or the other he quite dreaded the stiff salute and the "What will I be after doing now, sir?"

which he knew awaited him outside. Unfortunately Wilder, to whom he would have appealed, was now absent somewhere on duty or pleasure, and Verisopht was too shy to ask advice from any one else.

At last he found himself sitting disconsolately in the ante-room with only two of his brother officers. One was Captain Chutney he had already noticed at breakfast; the other was intent upon a newspaper. For a long time no one spoke, but eventually Captain Chutney marked Verisopht, and, bearing down upon him, opened fire.

"Were you ever in——"

A derisive laugh proceeded from behind the paper. Captain Chutney stopped short and glared fiercely for a few moments at the paper, and then repeated:

"Were you ever in In——"

Here there was a repetition of the laugh, and the slight was intensified by an expressive kick of the legs, as much as to say, "Oh, bother!"

Again did Captain Chutney break off

suddenly to glare witheringly at the insulting legs.

"Were you ever in India?" he at last said, accomplishing his query at the third time of asking.

Here the strange individual who had been interrupting rose up, dashed the paper on the table, and fled precipitately from the room.

"No, I never have; but I should like to go very much," said Verisopht in his blandest tones; for he saw that Captain Chutney's brow was ruffled, and he was anxious to dispel the cloud which had so suddenly settled there. This was not so easy, and it was not until Captain Chutney had muttered to himself two or three times over, "Calipash is an ass!" that he recovered sufficiently to proceed with the subject; but, having once got into it again, he soon warmed to his work, and poured broadside after broadside of Indian stories into Verisopht's open ears.

So gratified was the redoubtable Chutney at the way in which Verisopht swallowed these doses, that he at last asked if he could do anything for him.

"Well, there's my servant waiting outside," said Verisopht. "If you'd kindly tell me what I had better do with him, I should be very much obliged."

"He ought to be putting your things straight. Haven't you got a quarter yet?" asked Captain Chutney.

"No, I haven't."

"Well, send him to the Quarter-master —or stay, we'll go to him together, and I'll tell you about a struggle I once had with a tiger as we go along."

Under Captain Chutney's guidance, Verisopht was now conducted to the Quartermaster, from whom he received two small rooms, about ten feet square, with a table and two chairs in each; and then they went to the regimental tailor's shop — which wasn't a shop at all, but merely a room in a hut—where the giant was measured for a suit of plain clothes, and also one of mess livery.

All this took a considerable time, for

Captain Chutney's Indian stories were incessant. He was much addicted to drawing diagrams on the ground with his stick, to illustrate them, or stopping to show with great elaboration of pose and gesture how a sepoy crouched, a tiger sprang, or a jewelled Begum languished. Yes, how a Begum languished; for Captain Chutney's conquests in India were not only by the sword. As a languishing Begum Captain Chutney was particularly good. The consequence was that Verisopht, on his return, had only time to take a hurried lunch, and then hasten off to his afternoon drill with his mind so full of tigers, zemindars, and jewelled Begums, that Corporal Stickler could make nothing of him.

When Verisopht returned to his quarter after his drill, he found that the giant, assisted by Wilder's servant, had succeeded in imparting quite an air of comfort to the two small rooms. The crimson druggets were down, the portable furniture set up, and altogether, the tiny quarter, with a fire in the grate, and Mentor in his cage hanging up at the window, looked quite cosy and inviting. He spent some time in superintending and assisting in a few finishing touches, such as hanging up a few pictures of his relatives and one of the paternal dwelling against the wall, and fixing the coat-of-arms screen, with the son-of-a-sea-cook hornpipant and the pieman rampant, against the mantelpiece. He then dressed himself in plain clothes, so as to escape the embarrassing salutes of the soldiers, and sallied forth for a stroll through the camp. He would have liked a companion to point out the lions and explain novel sights to him, but at that late hour of the afternoon every officer had already gone off on his own business or pleasure, and Verisopht was forced to start on his voyage of discovery alone.

As he approached the adjoining lines, the noise he had heard in the early morning, and at intervals throughout the day, again filled the air.

"It's the most extraordinary thing. Soldiers must be very fond of pork; they seem to be killing pigs all day long here," thought Verisopht; and as he drew near to the spot whence the heart-rending sounds proceeded, he could not restrain himself from indignantly exclaiming aloud: " Oh ! why *don't* they put the poor thing out of its agony ?"

The next moment, on turning a corner of a hut, he came in full view of the Aberdeenshire Highlanders' parade-ground and of " the poor thing in its agony." Up and down the parade, strutting as only a piper can strut, was the Highland musician, while Colonel Angus MacTavish, his chief, sat in the garden of his hut, listening with gentle ecstasy to the dulcet notes.

As Verisopht gazed upon Colonel MacTavish's half-closed eyes and enraptured smile, he understood for the first time the exact meaning of the phrase, " the piping times of peace." Hurrying away from this peaceful scene, he pursued his walk through the camp with watchful and wondering eyes. Every moment something turned up worth staring at. A cavalry orderly trotting along with some order, the field-officer of the day going round the guards, attended by a lancer, a party returning from a funeral with the band playing merrily, a detachment of the Engineer train with their pontoons (which Verisopht took for the largest guns he had ever seen in all his life), and various other interesting sights, were all food for wonder and admiration.

In this way the afternoon was far spent by the time Verisopht returned to his quarters, and the remainder of the time before dressing for dinner was occupied in writing home to his parents. The letter was most voluminous, and contained, amongst other things, a full description of the sights he had seen that afternoon, a few extracts from Captain Chutney's stories, and a report of the wonderful phenomenon the night before, when it had been wet in one part of the camp and beautifully fine in another a quarter of a mile away.

By the time he had finished this, Wilder's servant came and showed the giant how to lay out his master's clothes for mess; and then Verisopht proceeded, somewhat nervously, to prepare himself for that rather trying ordeal, his first night at mess.

CHAPTER XI.

Is another important one—Sub-Lieutenant Boomershine's first night at mess—Two Heroes of Romance—Disagreeable position between two fires—The pure Pierian Spring—The Flowing Bowl—Our hero performs a double feat, and, in spite of sound practical advice from his friend Wilder, makes an enemy for life—He attends the "Symposium," and conducts himself with distinction at a performance held therein—For the last time he asks "Let me like a Soldier fall:" and they let him.

IT was with no small amount of trepidation that Verisopht dressed himself. With a beating heart he donned his spotless mess-jacket, and repaired to the ante-room. It was so full that his entrance was unobserved, and he sat unnoticed in a corner, to await the announcement of dinner, and to gaze with interest on the scene before him. It happened to be what is called "guest night," and there were several guests from other regiments, with a sprinkling of civilians in plain clothes; and there was a great deal of laughing and talking, and handing round of sherry and bitters by the mess-waiters. At last the dinner was announced, and all trooped across the camp-road into the mess-room, to the inspiriting strains of "The Roast Beef of Old England" from a portion of the band outside.

Verisopht modestly constituted himself the tail of the procession and eventually found himself one of the brightly-clad units sitting at the festive board. The rows of scarlet jackets, the glitter of silver plate, the sparkle of cut glass, the gorgeous liveries of the servants, the strains of military music, the buzz of conversation, above all the colours of the regiment crossed at the head of the room and displaying on their tattered folds many a glorious name—all made up a scene dazzling to his senses, accustomed as he had been all his life to the quiet of a country home.

Lost in admiration he was gazing about him when a voice on one side, saying, " Were you ever in the West Indies ?" and a half-defiant half-contemptuous snort on the other, recalled him to himself, and he found he was sitting between Captain Chutney on one side, and a Captain Calipash, who had exchanged from the West Indies, on the other. This last officer Verisopht recognised as the one who had behaved so unaccountably towards the Indian hero in the afternoon. His position between the two had been quite accidental on his part, but not so on theirs, and he now recollected that he had noticed them both hovering about him when he was looking for a seat at the table. The fact was both these gentlemen had recognised in him all those qualities which make up a good listener and an implicit believer; and, though politeness had occasionally afforded them the former, common sense had invariably stepped in and deprived them of the latter luxury. To secure his services, then, in both capacities during dinner was evidently the object with which each had seated himself beside our hero. The question; "Were you ever in the West Indies?" proceeded from Captain Calipash, the defiant snort from Captain Chutney.

"No, I never was," Verisopht replied in his politest tones. "But my mother's grandfather, Captain Peter Simple of the Royal Navy, once—"

"A wonderful country," interrupted Captain Calipash, who did not seem to care much about Verisopht's mother's grandfather—"a wonderful country, sir. 'The Land of the Guava and Turtle,' as I put it in a parody I once wrote on Lord Byron's beautiful lines:

'Know ye the land where the cypress and myrtle'—

You recollect the rest, I dare say—commencement of 'The Bride of Abydos,' you know. My effusion appeared in the

'Tobago Tickler,' and created some sensation, I can assure you. I'll just give you the first stanza:

"'Know ye the land where the guava and turtle
  Are toothsome when eaten with juice of the lime,
 Where the maw of the vulture, the fancy most fertile
  Would fail to do justice to subjects so prime?
 Oh, know ye the land of the sugar-cane sweet,
 The tamarind so pungent, the land-crab so fleet;
 Where the soothing mosquito flies into your room,
 And lulls you to sleep through the night's dreary gloom;
 Where the gentle tarantula creeps up the stairs,
 And the warmth of your bed condescendingly shares;
 Where the centipede hides midst the folds of your suit,
 And the scorpion ensconces himself in your boot;
 While the lithe rattlesnake in affectionate coils
 Cheers the virtuous planter amidst all his toils?
 Know ye this land where these pleasures sublime
 Lend a charm to existence in its sunny clime?
 Oh, know ye the joys and delights to be got
 From sangarree, cassareepe, hot pepper-pot?
 Say ye, sweet as Old England's no lasses can be—
 Nay, sweeter by far are *mo*lasses to me.'

Now what do you think of that?" asked Captain Calipash, his voice still trembling with the emotion produced by the pathos of some of the lines.

"B-e-a-u-tiful!" replied Verisopht.

"Now there you're *quite* right," said Captain Calipash, as if Verisopht had been strikingly original in his praise; "that's *just* the term. It *is* beautiful. And yet it inadequately conveys a notion of the charms of those enchanting isles. You can't help being a poet in that country, sir. Everything appeals to the poetic side of your nature. I'll give you an instance of this. Walking through a cane-field one day, with my favourite rattle in my pocket, I was—"

"I beg your pardon," said Verisopht, "like a policeman?"

"No, no, no," said Captain Calipash, laughing at his innocence; "a rattle—a rattlesnake, you know. Well, with my favourite rattle in my pocket—"

"Dear me!" gasped Verisopht; "I thought they were such fearfully venomous creatures."

"So they are—so they are, my dear sir,

in their *natural* state. And so are tigers, and yet we cherish the species under the name of cats. No, a tame—a *properly* tamed rattlesnake is by no means an unpleasant pet. This little fellow of mine used to go out into the woods during the day, but never omitted to return punctually at nightfall. In fact, this gave rise to another poetical effusion of mine, quite a domestic little gem:

"'Mary, call the rattle home.'

Pretty idea, wasn't it? Well, to resume, walking through a cane-field one day with my favourite rattle in my tail-pocket, I was struck with the beauty of the landscape, and, cutting a piece of sugar-cane, I sat down to enjoy the view before me, and at the same time to sip some of nature's sweets literally. Unfortunately, I sat on my rattle! Now, sir, we all know a worm when trodden upon will turn, and on the same principle, a rattle, *even a tame* rattle, when sat upon, will resent the familiarity, not to say discomfort, of the proceeding.

My senses reeled in a fine frenzy, and I gnashed my teeth until the juice from my sugar-cane ran down my throat in a delicious stream. Well, sir, what between the two sensations — sugar-cane, rattlesnake—a mad, resistless spirit of poetry evolved itself from my inner consciousness, and seizing my notebook—always travel about with a notebook in a country like that—I dashed off the following:

ODE TO A SUGAR-CANE.

" 'Oh, were I a boy to be flogged once again,
   I'd say, "Let it be with the sweet sugar-cane."
   For though it would smart, I would think with sly laughter
   Of the saccharine joys it would yield me soon after.
   A meekness and gentle submission I'd show
   To authority's rule, ne'er surpassed here below.
   Though *kissing* the rod may be noble and good,
   I'd be still more forgiving—I'd *eat* it, I would.'

Don't you call that wonderful?" said Captain Calipash. "Isn't that poetry, sir— poetry bubbling — *bubbling!* squirting— that's the word—irresistibly squirting from the pure Pierian spring? If it hadn't been for the rattle, that forcible, that ecstatic reminder of my schooldays would never have pierced my soul; and if it hadn't been for the sugar-cane, I could never have applied that sweet and touching lesson of submission which it can afford under peculiar circumstances. Now, to such an extent had I tamed this rat—"

For some time Verisopht had noticed, as far as his attention had been allowed to wander, that Captain Chutney, on the other side, had been fussing and fuming, beating a devil's tattoo with his feet, unbuttoning his waistcoat and buttoning it up again, and acting generally in a way denoting great perturbation of spirit. But at this point, as if no longer able to control himself, Verisopht felt him rapping double knocks against his ribs with his elbow.

"I beg your pardon," said Captain Chutney in a low tone of voice, "but I merely wished to tell you that all Captain Calipash's statements must be received with the greatest caution. It is in no unfriendly spirit towards Calipash that I say this, but merely in the interests of truth.

Now, what *is* the use of a fellow telling a lot of twisters like that? The only wonder to me is that they don't twist the very teeth out of his head. He *must* know no creature can swallow them. And the worst of it is, he not only makes himself ridiculous and contemptible, but, by George! he prevents other people, who have really something rational to talk about, from getting a word in. Now I was just going to tell you, when he regularly pinned you by the ear, about an adventure I once had 'up country.' We had been pig-sticking, sir—fox-hunting! pish! If fox-hunting be the sport of kings, pig-sticking is the sport of emperors. Well, sir, my horse having been gored by a rare old tusker, I dismounted, and, leaving him in the care of the horse-boy, I started off with the intention of walking through the jungle to the cantonment. Well, sir, I hadn't proceeded more than a mile, when all of a sudden I found myself face to face with a man-eater, which had been the terror of the neighbourhood for months. There he crouched, the monarch of the jungle, making a light repast, just as you or I might have done, off a few natives. Ha! ha! ha! It was no laughing matter, though — by Jove! it wasn't, sir! Dropping the thigh-bone he was in the act of crunching, the animal threw himself back on his haunches ready for a spring. Had my nerves failed me, had my hand trembled, had I quailed for a moment, I had been a dead man. But, sir, I did neither the first, the second, nor the third. Luckily I still carried the spear used for pig-sticking, and just at the moment when he was about to spring, quick as lightning I planted it between his shoulders; and, using it as a leaping-pole, I pledge you my sacred word of honour as an officer and a gentleman, I flew several—"

Here Captain Calipash nudged Verisopht.

"I beg your pardon," said Captain Calipash, in confidential tones; "I think I heard Chutney pledging his sacred word of honour as an officer and a gentleman.

Now, I should be very sorry to disparage a brother officer; but I think I am only right in placing you on your guard against old Chutney. He is well known as the Ananias of the British Army, and 'I pledge you my sacred word of honour as an officer and a gentleman' is his invariable prelude to the biggest—well, well, I don't wish to say Chutney is a wilful perverter of the truth. It's a disease, sir, with him —a disease for which he is no more accountable than if he caught the yellow fever. I pity poor Chutney."

Although the subject of this interruption could not hear what was said, it was quite enough, or rather too much for him, that his listener's attention had been withdrawn from his story at its culminating point.

"There are some people," said Captain Chutney, looking straight at the candelabra in front of him, and speaking with suppressed fury, " who hate to hear anything but their own vapid stories."

" There are some people," said Captain Calipash, looking with equal fixedness and ferocity at a silver vase, "whose stories are open to a much more serious charge than vapidity."

After this Captains Calipash and Chutney breathed hard, and Verisopht looked, with a troubled countenance, from one to the other. Captain Chutney, from India, was, as a rule, bright red, and Captain Calipash, from the West Indies, a pale yellow; and Verisopht noticed that during this passage of arms the former deepened into a vivid beetroot shade, while the latter faded away to a delicate lemon tint. Verisopht was pained beyond measure by the *contretemps*.

"Mr. Wilder's compliments, sir, and he wishes to have the pleasure of taking wine with you," said a servant, at the same time filling up our hero's champagne glass.

Verisopht was as pleased at the interruption as at the attention, and, looking up the table, saw Wilder at the other end nodding to him and holding up his glass. Verisopht did the same, and drank off the contents as he saw Wilder do.

"Capital old custom," said Captain Calipash, who now seemed better; "I am sorry it has gone out of date. We always revive it, however, in the case of an officer's first or last night at mess. Allow me to have the pleasure. Waiter, fill Mr. Boomershine's glass."

Verisopht drank with Captain Calipash. Then Captain Chutney asked to have the pleasure; then Captain This, and Major That, and Mr. So-and-So all asked to have the pleasure too.

Every one drank wine with Verisopht; and by the time he had "hob-nobbed" with all in turn he had imbibed quite as much as, if not rather more than, was good for him.

There were other exciting influences at work besides the champagne—the novelty of the scene, the sense of suddenly-acquired independence and manhood, the martial strains of music, and the wonderful tales of heroism poured into his ears by Captains Chutney and Calipash. These two rivals were at him the whole of dinner-time, and when their stories clashed, which was of frequent occurrence, owing to Verisopht's inability to listen to both at the same time, they glared across him at each other with a withering scorn and contempt which almost made Verisopht shiver in his seat.

Altogether, by the time the dessert period of the dinner had arrived, Verisopht was considerably exhilarated.

"Mr. Vice," said an officer sitting at the head of the table, as soon as the after-dinner wine had gone round and every glass had been filled—"The Queen."

"Gentlemen," said the officer at the bottom of the table—"The Queen."

Then everybody muttered "The Queen" to himself, and drank off the contents of his glass, while simultaneously the band struck up the National Anthem.

Verisopht was at first lost in admiration of the President's and the Vice-President's eloquence, but when the strains of "God save the Queen" fell on his ears this feeling gave way to one of enthusiastic loyalty, and he drank to Her Majesty in a bumper.

From this point our hero seemed to enter upon a strange and bewildering sort of dual existence. There seemed to be two Verisopht Boomershines: one, the modest, retiring Verisopht he had known from his birth upward; the other, a talkative creature with a loud laugh and a disposition to run all his words into one another; and at times a sudden return to his original self, with the other Verisopht's laugh still ringing in his ears, was disconcerting in the extreme. Gradually, however, the former existence became completely merged in the latter, and Verisopht launched out into long anecdotes and stories which, if devoid of the startling incidents of Captains Chutney and Calipash's narratives, still equalled, if not surpassed them in length and detail. As a talker, however, Verisopht did not find that favour in the eyes of Captains Chutney and Calipash that, as a listener, he had previously enjoyed. Their attention to his remarks was rather *distrait*, as they were either still struggling with the recollection, mirthful or otherwise, of their own last stories, or concocting the material for their next.

After the wine had gone round several times there was a general adjournment to the ante-room and billiard-room. Verisopht happened to follow those going to the latter, and, taking a seat, watched the game of pool going on with considerable interest, and also listened with great attention to the jargon about " Red on white ; yellow's your player in hand ;" " One life off white," &c. After being a looker-on for some time, he was seized with a desire to become a player. What a free-and-easy, dashing sort of a thing, becoming the cloth he wore, it would be to play at billiards and smoke a cigar at the same time ! Should he perform this spirited feat ? Yes, his mind was made up, and he took a cigar from a waiter and a ball for the new pool, just commencing, from the marker. All the skill he possessed with the cue had been acquired on a bagatelle-board at home in exciting matches with his sisters, and he was anxious for laurels gathered from fresh fields. There were serious drawbacks to his play, however, in the present instance, and the greatest of all, perhaps, was that cigar. It was always creating a sensation by dropping on the table, or sending its smoke into his eyes just as he was aiming at a ball, or down his throat just as he was going to make a remark, or, worst of all, he would sometimes in his confusion, and not much to its abatement either, put the wrong end into his mouth. At last, by way of a change, it fell under, instead of on the table, and rolled away, greatly to his relief. This did not lead, however, to any great improvement in his play, and each of his strokes was generally followed by an announcement from the marker that "there was another life off yaller." Acting steadily on this principle, it was not long before the final announcement from the marker that "yaller was dead" put a stop to the erratic wanderings of that ball about the table, and Verisopht subsided into the more suitable but less prominent part of a looker-on—not before, though, he had made an enemy for life of Captain Spott-Browne, the great pool-player of the regiment, whom he had "sold" twice by the eccentricity of his play.

Of course Hooky Wilder had been present all through the game, assisting Verisopht with such sound and practical pieces of advice, as "Chalk the handle and hit hard, old fellow,"—"Hole the red and swallow your cue;" but, curiously enough, without any very brilliant results. That volatile young officer, as soon as the pool was concluded, proposed an adjournment of such as desired it to the "Symposium."

"Will you come, Boomershine?" he asked.

"I should be very happy, but I don't know what a 'symposium' is."

"Well, you see, one can't kick up much row in the ante-room, for the old hands and fellows playing cards don't like it, so we've got hold of a spare quarter, and have shoved a piano into it, and a lot of sofas and armchairs; and you may go and stand on your head and yell blue murder for an hour if you like, with no one to interfere with you."

These two advantages were not to be gainsaid, and as Verisopht followed a noisy party of youngsters out into the open air he seemed to be practising his steps for the first part of the performance.

The "Symposium" was, as Wilder had said, merely an unoccupied quarter fitted up as a lounging-room, where the younger and more boisterous spirits of the regiment could disport themselves to the top of their bent, unchecked by older hands and cooler heads.

The proceedings were conducted in a spirit of the wildest revelry, which, as Hooky Wilder was a sort of master of the ceremonies, was only to be expected.

"Now then, gentlemen," said Hooky, "the entertainments will commence with an overture by the entire band. Can you play the scuttleoon, Boomershine?"

"No; I don't think I ever saw one; and, indeed——"

'Oh, well, it's very easy; you'll soon

pick it up," said Wilder, handing the coal-scuttle to Verisopht. "You just turn the beggar up and welt him with the poker at intervals. Now then, Buffer, you play the tongbone. Capital tongbone player," whispered Wilder to Verisopht, as he handed Buffer the pair of tongs; "performs with great expression, especially when he jams his knuckles in his instrument."

The remaining instruments of the orchestra consisted of the piano, a banjo, a set of bones, and an empty Bass's pale-ale bottle, which Wilder called a bassoon, and was played on the objects nearest to the performer's hand.

After Wilder, as leader, had requested Verisopht to give them a key-note by striking Q flat on the scuttleoon, he gave the signal to commence, and the overture was rattled through with great spirit. As to Verisopht, he performed his part so well as to lead, by universal acclamation, to the distinction of being crowned with his own instrument.

"Is Boomershine here?" said a voice, as the door opened at this juncture, and Captain Chutney's rubicund countenance loomed through the smoke.

"Yes," said Wilder. "Come in, Chutney; but be good enough to leave India on the door-mat."

This sentiment was heartily and generally endorsed.

Captain Chutney, though very peppery and hot, evidently looked upon Wilder as a privileged being, particularly in the symposium, where Wilder reigned supreme, and it was in sorrow rather than in anger that he said :

"My dear fellow, if you don't care for what is universally allowed to be the brightest jewel in the British crown, there are others, perhaps, who do."

Here Captain Chutney looked with a longing eye and an itching tongue on Verisopht.

"Is my authority paramount in this symposium, or is it not?" asked Wilder in mock heroic tones.

General cheering announced that in the opinion of the meeting the former was decidedly the case.

"Very well then—am or am I not the founder of this glorious Institution?"

"You are!" resounded on all sides.

"Very well then. Being the founder and the president of this Institution, let it be understood that the following inscription is written in letters of gold over the portal:

"'Lasciate ogni speranza voi ch'entrate,'

which, not being Hindustani, Captain Chutney, I'll translate for your benefit, as follows:

"'All you that enter here leave shop behind.'

Now, gentlemen, what's the next thing on the programme?"

On this a gentleman volunteered a song with a chorus, and while it was being sung and the attention of the company taken up with "ri-tooral-looraloo ri-tooral-lay," Captain Chutney managed to get Verisopht into a corner, and in low tones recited something about an alligator in his compound at Ahmednuggur.

He had just got into the jaws, and the most thrilling part of the story in connection with his miraculous extrication therefrom, was only requiring the usual sacred pledge of his word of honour as an officer and a gentleman, to give it the finishing touch, when the door was opened and a voice was heard saying—

"Is Boomershine here?"

Captain Chutney stuck hard and fast in the alligator's jaws, and his brow grew black.

"That man's pertinacity in persecuting every new comer is—is—hang it! it is beyond human conception," muttered Captain Chutney in tones of considerable irritation, not to say suppressed fury.

"Come in, Calipash," said Wilder. "Boomershine's here all right."

Captain Calipash entered. The atmosphere of the room was so thick with smoke that it was a few moments before he could distinguish the different forms. His face suddenly brightened up.

"Aha! there you are, Boomershine. I've been looking everywhere——"

His face suddenly fell, and his complexion, as before, faded away to a delicate lemon tint.

"Really," murmured Captain Calipash to himself, "the blind fatuity of that insufferable bore, which leads him to imagine that his palpable perversions of truth can take in any one would be beyond belief, were it not so constantly before one's senses. Oh, it would be amusing, positively amusing, you know, if it were not so confoundedly enraging."

The result of the simultaneous presence of these two gentlemen was that Verisopht enjoyed a complete immunity from the attentions of either.

Vocal music, combined with liquid refreshment, was now the order of the evening, and Verisopht was soon called upon for a song. To the astonishment of the company he required no pressing whatever; but of course they did not know that he was primed to the very throat with "Let me like a Soldier fall," and had been for some time anxiously awaiting an opportunity to let it off.

Expectation was on tip-toe. Verisopht had cleared his throat preparatory to uplifting his voice, when a knock at the door interrupted the harmony.

"Here, hold hard, Boomershine," said Wilder. "Nothing like getting off with a good start. Come in, can't you."

The door was opened, and a corporal of the regimental guard, fully accoutred, entered with a salute.

"Major Grizzle's compliments to you, Mr. Wilder, sir, and he says, would you be good enough to leave off singing, as you're keeping the whole lines awake?"

"This is extremely tantalising," said Wilder, "just as we were going to hear the song of the evening—beautiful song. But never shall it be said of this symposium, of which I am the founder, and you, gentlemen, the supporters, that it was 'subversive of good order and military discipline.' There is nothing for us but to obey. Boomershine, you must bottle up your harmony until another occasion."

Very great disappointment was expressed on all sides, and no one was more disappointed than Verisopht himself, who felt that he had never been in such voice before, or so ripe for a song.

"Stay," said Wilder, as he tore off a corner of a bit of music. "I'll write the Major a line, and perhaps he'll relent."

"DEAR MAJOR,
 "You will be conferring a great and much appreciated favour on a hard-worked and deserving body of men, if you will, with your characteristic affability, allow us to sing one more song.
 "Believe me, my dear Major,
  "Very truly yours,
   "R. C. WILDER.
"The Symposium,
"In the Small Hours."

The corporal was despatched with this

document, and after a few moments of expectation on the part of the company in general, and of the keenest anxiety on the part of Verisopht in particular, returned with the following scribbled on the back:

"Sing your song, and go to the devil. I wish you'd exchange into another regiment, and then there would be some peace in this.

"HARDY GRIZZLE."

"That's all right," said Wilder triumphantly. "Now, Boomershine, old fellow, tune up and fire away."

Taking up his position in the middle of the room, our hero quavered forth, with flushed cheeks and a slight thickness of speech, the song he had so often practised in the bosom of his family for the future delectation of his brother officers, and that they appreciated his efforts was evident from the way in which they held their sides and crammed their handkerchiefs into their mouths. These manifestations of delight, however flat-

'HE WOULD BE A SOLDIER!'
'Then let me like a soldier fall.'

Drawn by R. Caldecott.]

tering they might have been to the vocalist, were utterly lost on Verisopht, whose eyes were turned feelingly up to the ceiling from the commencement of the performance to the *finale*, which, as it should have been, was the most thrilling part. With his left hand on the spot where a rather hazy knowledge of anatomy led him to believe his heart lay, and his right pointing upwards (as enjoined by both Fanny and Carry), he sang the last verse, and as the concluding words, "then like a s-o-o-oldier fall," escaped his lips, a sofa-cushion skimmed across the room, and, cutting his legs clean from under him, made him suit his action to his words in the most natural way possible, amidst the deafening plaudits of his audience.

Verisopht recovered his perpendicular, and tried to look dignified; but it is a hard thing to stand on your dignity when you can't stand on your legs; and there was, in truth, but little dignity about the proceeding as he sank to the sofa smiling inanely.

An hour or so afterwards Mentor looked down from his cage in speechless wonder at a sad sight. Not a precept did he utter, not a moral sentiment escaped his beak; but, with his head very much on one side, he gazed blankly down on a laughing group of subalterns round a limp figure, which at one moment was pugnacious and offering to fight the assembly collectively, the next friendly and shaking hands all round, then sentimental and easily moved to tears, then merry and laughing wildly, and, finally, sleepy, in which stage it was tucked comfortably in bed and left.

Mentor shook his head sadly, and croaked out, "Evil com——" Here he sank off into a doze.

CHAPTER XII.

Remorse—Repentance and soda-water—Agonising doubts—Determination to desert—Breakfast and change of mind.

—" MUNICATIONS corrupt good manners," said Mentor, taking up the thread of his discourse, on being awakened by the drums and fifes playing the *reveillée* about two hours afterwards.

Verisopht, too, was aroused by the same sounds. Oh, the horrid awakening to consciousness!—the parched mouth, the racking head, the burning recollection of what he had done, the torturing doubts as to what he might not have done in those hours of madness and folly! Ther, too,

Mentor's utterances smote on his heart with the force of a sledge-hammer. That virtuous bird was moralising freely.

Verisopht had not been awake very long when the giant entered the room as softly as it is in the nature of six-foot-two in hobnailed ammunition boots to do.

In fear and trembling Verisopht awaited his opening remark. Perhaps he had heard all about it, and was even now come to throw up his situation with indignant scorn.

But no, thank Heaven, he could have heard nothing. His demeanour was as deferential as it could be, as he announced, "The recruits is fallen in, and it's time to get up for drill, sir."

"What time is it?" asked Verisopht.

It was the first time he had spoken, and his tongue resounded in his own head like the clapper of a bell.

"Just gone six, sir."

Verisopht groaned. He felt that to stand with his head erect, feet closed at an angle of sixty degrees, hands close to his sides, palms to the front, and thumbs one inch in rear of the seams of his trousers, as Corporal Stickler would direct him, would be a physical impossibility.

"The recruits is out on the square, sir," said the giant suggestively.

"Out on the square!" The words sounded familiar, and set themselves to a tune in his head mingled with a jingling of a piano and glasses, and shouting, and the fumes of liquor. Then he hazily recollected that he was thinking of a chorus he had heard in that dreadful symposium, "Act on the square, boys! act on the square!" What a capital sentiment he had thought it then as he had roared it out at the top of his voice; but what a ghastly mockery, what a downright impossibility would be any attempt of his to act on the square now as he should be doing!

A knock at the door rekindled Verisopht's apprehensions.

The Adjutant, perhaps, to take away his sword and place him under arrest; or Captain Chutney or Captain Calipash taking the earliest opportunity of cancelling the friendly advances of the previous day, and repudiating all further acquaintanceship with him; or Wilder, come to say he could not have him in his company any longer.

His last conjecture was nearest the mark, for if not the master, it was the man.

"Mr. Wilder, sir," said that officer's servant as he entered, "said I was to bring you this the first thing before you went out to drill."

The man bore in one hand a large tumbler containing the juice of a freshly-squeezed lemon and a large lump of ice; in the other a bottle of soda-water, which he at once proceeded to open.

"There, sir, Mr. Wilder says if you take that, and have your tub after, you'll be all right for your drill."

As Verisopht raised his fevered head and stretched out his hand to take the proffered cup, he was conscious of a twinkle in the man's eye, though the rest of his features were composed and staid, which

Drawn by R Caldecott]

"HE WOULD BE A SOLDIER."

"There, sir, Mr. Wilder says if you take that, and have your tub after, you'll be all right for your drill"

was very disconcerting. Not disconcerting enough, though, to prevent his raising the tumbler to his parched lips and draining every drop of the delicious liquid.

"The recruits is fallen in this ten minutes, and the Adjutant's a-waitin' on the square, sir," said the attendant giant, popping his head in at the door.

The last announcement—"the Adjutant's a-waitin'"—brought Verisopht out of his bed in the twinkling of an eye. To him the Adjutant was a very important personage, and to keep him waiting was not to be thought of. The Adjutant himself, apparently, had no intention either of being kept waiting, for at that very moment the jingle of armed heels resounded through the little passage, and with a premonitory tap at the door, he entered the room.

"Well, young man, you ought to have been out on the square half an hour ago, eh?"

"I really am very sorry indeed," said Verisopht; "but the fact is, I did not feel very well."

"Were you at what that fellow Wilder calls his 'symposium' last night?"

"Yes."

"Ah, that accounts for it. Well, never mind the drill this morning," said the Adjutant good-naturedly; "you don't look up to very much. Tumble into bed again, and we'll make up for it another time." And after bestowing a few whistles on Mentor, he walked out, grunting something very uncomplimentary about Wilder's "symposium."

Verisopht was not long in literally following the advice of tumbling into bed, and in a few moments he was sound asleep.

When he awoke two or three hours later, he found Hooky Wilder standing over his bed.

"You're a nice young man, *you* are. Do you recollect what you did last night?"

"I recollect singing a song."

"Ah! but after that?"

Verisopht confessed, with burning blushes, that after that all was buried in oblivion.

"Well, you don't recollect, I suppose, serenading the Colonel outside his quarters?"

" N-o-o."

"Nor saying, when he shoved his head out of the window, 'Now, then, Old Fireworks, tip us a song?'"

Verisopht turned his face to the wall and groaned.

"Nor throwing stones at his door?"

Verisopht's head disappeared under the bedclothes.

"Nor offering to fight him for a five-pound note—perhaps you don't recollect *that?*"

Verisopht slid down to the bottom of the bed, taking along with him the bolster, which he clutched to his bosom in his agony of mind.

"And then when he wouldn't fight calling him an old coward?"

On this there were violent struggles under the bedclothes, as if the unhappy young man were trying to cut his throat with the bolster.

"And then running at him with your

head down and butting him in the waist coat? Come, *that must* have impressed itself on your brain."

A convulsive movement under the bed-clothes and a few muffled groans were the only response.

"Well, I'll tell you what's the best thing to be done—but I can't give confidential advice through half a dozen blankets and sheets."

Verisopht's face emerged from the bed-clothes, presenting a picture of abject despair.

"I shall desert, and go to the back-woods of America, I shall."

"No, no—much better stay here. It's all right. Old Rooteen didn't see who it was," said Wilder, who, arch-tormentor as he was, was touched by Verisopht's woful countenance. "Just let the whole thing slide, and don't go apologising or anything of that sort. If *you* keep quiet *he* will. Now get up and have your breakfast. I'm off for mine, and I'll order you a hot devil."

Verisopht was a little comforted by Wilder's concluding remarks; but still it was with a heavy heart and an aching head that he proceeded to dress himself. At the mess he found his breakfast awaiting him; but the "devil," though prepared by Wilder himself, was a devil that failed to tempt.

All day he went about his duties in a limp and dejected manner, and his feeble attempts to hold up his head and to spring up smartly at the last sound of the word "'shun!" nearly broke Corporal Stickler's heart.

As he was returning from his last drill in the afternoon Wilder met him, and was so touched by his seedy appearance that he took him forthwith out in his dog-cart for a country drive. The fresh air brightened him up a little, and before they had gone many miles he confided to Wilder that never again as long as he lived would he drink one drop more than was good for him.

"I'll tell you what I'll do, Wilder; I'll go to my room every night after mess, like Slowcock, and study for the Staff College.

Don't you think that would be a capital plan?"

"My dear Boomershine, I shall be more in a position to give you some practical advice on that subject when we arrive at the summit of yonder eminence."

So saying, Wilder urged his steed forward, and drove to the top of one of the Surrey hills, whence a view of the surrounding country for many miles could be obtained. Here he pulled up, and, using his whip as a showman's wand, spoke with a solemnity which deeply impressed his companion.

"You say you mean to go to the Staff College. If you carry out that intention the theatre of your whole career as a soldier lies at your feet. There, on the left, are the huts of the camp, where you are at present acquiring the rudiments of a military education under Corporal Stickler's tuition——"

"And yours too," said Verisopht gratefully. "I'm sure I'm indebted to you for—"

"Well, well, perhaps I *have* enlightened

you on a few points; but let that pass," said Wilder, with characteristic modesty. "As I said before, there is the camp, where you now are. There, amongst those woods, is Sandhurst, where you will be, and where you will renew for the space of two years some of the sweetest pleasures of your boyhood in the shape of Euclid and algebra. Then where, in the natural course of events, do you think you will go to next?"

"Where?" asked Verisopht, deeply interested.

"There—to that red-brick establishment with the gables, in the far distance. And that, my dear Boomershine, is the—Lunatic Asylum."

"Dear me!" gasped Verisopht.

"Then the last and final scene in this sad and degraded career lies in that direction, where you see those white dots scattered about."

"And what is that?"

"Woking Cemetery," said Wilder, in a sepulchral tone of voice

Verisopht was inexpressibly shocked.

" And you mean to say that is———"

" Invariably the end of men who go to the Staff College. I have lost some of my best friends that way." And Wilder turned away and held his handkerchief up to his face for a few brief moments.

Verisopht descended the hill a wiser and sadder man.* He recovered his spirits during the drive home, and, what was better for his health, got up a tremendous appetite for dinner. After mess he retired to rest at an early hour, strong in his recently-made resolution never to be led into any excesses in future.

* It is right to inform the reader that Lieutenant Wilder had himself been to the Staff College, from which institution his overweening love of practical joking had speedily secured him the honour of a graceful and not wholly voluntary retirement; consequently his opinions on this subject must be received with grains of allowance.

CHAPTER XIII.

Is perhaps the most thrilling in the whole book—Our hero is pleased to find that he commands the respect of his brothers-in-arms—He gladdens the martial soul of Corporal Stickler—He applies a highly complimentary term to his commanding officer with an awful result—He drives a worthy old soldier clean out of his mind, and nearly goes out of his own—He contemplates suicide—When night is darkest dawn is nearest—Explanation.

"WHAT'S the meaning of the word 'duffer,' Wilder?" asked Verisopht, the following morning, as he happened to meet that individual.

"Why? has any one been calling you one?"

"Well, I heard a lot of them saying in the mess-room, when they didn't know I was near, that I was an 'out-and-out duffer.'"

"I must congratulate you, my dear Boomershine," said Wilder warmly. "It is seldom that a young officer commands the respect of his brothers-in-arms in so short a time as you evidently have done. Duffer is a term implying unusual skill and proficiency in most pursuits, combined with consummate tact and ready wit in emergencies."

Verisopht never felt prouder in his life than when he heard this definition; and he went off to his drill with an elasticity of step and stateliness of carriage that gladdened the martial soul of Drill-Corporal Stickler. As Praxiteles or Canova might have regarded the rough-hewn block of marble gradually assuming beauty of form and outline under the skilful manipulation of the chisel, so did Corporal Stickler regard the gradual transformation, under his auspices, of a raw recruit into a smart soldier.

But Corporal Stickler's satisfaction did not rest here. All through the lesson Verisopht held up his head, threw out his chest, and "carried back" his hands, in the splendid style befitting one who had earned for himself the proud title of "duffer," a person possessing "unusual skill and proficiency in most pursuits, combined with consummate tact and ready wit in emergencies." Verisopht was receiving the congratulations of Corporal Stickler at the conclusion of the drill, when an orderly came up with a message from the Adjutant that the Colonel wished to see him at once in the orderly-room.

The summons was startling, and a little of the "consummate tact and ready wit" seemed to desert him in this "emergency;" but he soon recovered his composure, and hastened to obey the mandate.

The important business of the morning was evidently over as he entered, and the orderly-room was filled with officers laughing with military precision at their Colonel's jokes. The great man was in high feather. The two-years-and-a-half struggle with the War Office over eleven pence three farthings had come to a glorious termination that very morning, and, flushed with victory, he was letting off a rapid succession of his primest old jokes in honour of the occasion. In justice to Colonel Rooteen, it must be explained that principle, not parsimony, was at the root of his gratification. After the Colonel himself, who always laughed very much, the mirth and the rank were in an inverse ratio—the greater the one, the less the other. After each joke the senior Major said "Ha, ha!" the junior Major, "Ha, ha, ha!" the Captains laughed with apparent relish; the Lieutenants roared; and the Sub-lieutenants screamed.

"Well, Mr. Boomershine," said the Colonel, beaming with good-temper (eleven pence three farthings was not to be got out of the War Office every day in the week), "I just wished to see you, and to judge for myself whether you are making any progress in your drill. When right's in front what's the pivot?"*

" Right, sir."

"No, not *right* exactly," said the Colonel. " Try again."

" Left, sir."

" Very good, indeed. I am rejoiced to see that you are mastering these abstruse details so ably. There is a great improvement, too, in your carriage, even in this short time; and I am glad to find that you are so attentive and anxious to acquire a knowledge of your profession. It is very commendable — very commendable indeed."

" I am indeed obliged to you, sir, for your good opinion," said Verisopht, " and, coming from a duffer like you, they——"

" Zounds and fury!" ejaculated Colonel Rooteen, turning an apoplectic purple, and springing up to his feet. He then tried to speak, but wrath choked his utterance.

* Now obsolete.

Verisopht looked aghast, first at his enraged chief, then all round him. Captain Chutney had turned quite pale—a performance he had always been thought incapable of; Captain Calipash looked as if he had swallowed one of his own West Indian stories by mistake and was fast choking; while blank astonishment was depicted in every other face. As to the orderly-room sergeant, who had grown grey in the service, and sat at a little table by himself making up returns all day, he stared idiotically for a few moments, and then murmured, as one in a dream:

"For five-and-twenty years countin' boy-service, I've been——"

"Leave the room, sergeant!" roared the Colonel.

"—in this regiment," went on the sergeant opening a cupboard-door and feebly trying to walk through.

"Lead him to the door!" shouted the Colonel. "He's gone mad, and, zounds! no wonder!"

"—and never have I heard tell of such a thing," continued the poor man, in weak tones, as he was being led from the room, " as the junior——"

The remainder of the sentence was lost in the passage. The shock had been too much for that well-disciplined mind; reason had evidently, for the time, fled.

"Now, sir," said the Colonel, in most terrific tones, " wha-wha-wha-what have you got to say for yourself?"

" Please, sir——"

" Not a word, sir! not a word! you have committed yourself quite sufficiently already. What have you got to say, eh?"

" Really, sir—I'm sure sir——"

"Silence, sir, I tell you, when you dare to address me! Go to your room, sir, under arrest—close arrest, and I shall try you by court-martial. Away with you, sir!"

Verisopht never knew how he got from the orderly-room to his own quarters; but he found himself soon after lying on his bed, groaning and twining his fingers in his hair.

This, then, was the end of all his military aspirations—trial by court-martial and ignominious expulsion from the service! Was it for this he had thrown up fronts of Vauban's first system in the kitchen garden? What would his father and mother and brothers and sisters say? What would Aunt Millicent think? And what for? What had he done to bring all this upon himself? Simply nothing that he could think of. He had merely applied a highly complimentary term to his commanding officer, and forthwith this storm had burst on his devoted head. Conscious innocence, however, heightened, rather than allayed, Verisopht's anguish of spirit; and the longer he cogitated over his trials the lower he descended into the depths of despair.

He had just arrived at that point in these gloomy depths when *felo de se* seemed about the pleasantest release from his troubles that he could devise, when the sound of laughter jarred upon his feelings, and in another moment Wilder rushed into the room in a state of hilarity which contrasted forcibly with the other's misery. And what was very unfeeling indeed about Wilder was that the more wretched Verisopht looked, the louder he laughed.

"It's the richest thing I ever heard of. I have only just come back from a court-martial in the other lines, and heard what took place in the orderly-room. It's all right, old fellow. I've explained the whole thing to old Rooteen, and he says that you are to go and see him at once in the orderly-room."

"Now, young gentleman," said the Colonel, when Verisopht made his appearance; "you are, of course, released from arrest. It was all a mistake. But let me give you a word of advice. Mr. Wilder is a very volatile young officer; and if you take all his jokes and nonsense for gospel, this won't be your last scrape. There, now come and have some lunch with me at my quarters. Stay; perhaps you had better embody your reply in the form of an official and——Dear me! dear me! we are all slaves of habit! Come along. Time, tide, and Mrs Rooteen, wait for no man."

CHAPTER XIV.

Church parade—Pride has a fall—The church militant—A Sunday in quarters.

THE following day was a Sunday, and Verisopht was allowed the unspeakable honour of dressing in full uniform and marching to church with the regiment. Anxiously watching how his pupil acquitted himself on this, his first *début* on parade, was Corporal Stickler, who walked alongside the regiment, carrying a pace-stick, with which he occasionally admonished a recruit when he happened to lose that magic and always-being-lost "light touch below the elber."

The distance from the parade ground to the church-door was only about a hundred and fifty yards, yet the few moments occupied in accomplishing it were amongst the proudest of Verisopht's life. He had never marched to military music before, and every tap of the big drum found a responsive echo in his heart. His martial bearing quite delighted Corporal Stickler, who felt that he was being done credit to. With head erect and eyes that scorned the ground, our hero marched proudly on, his soul afire with warlike thoughts. He had won the Victoria Cross and a field-marshal's *bâton*, received the thanks of both Houses of Parliament, been offered a peerage, and was just fixing upon a well-sounding title, when there was a clatter and rattle, and Verisopht found himself embracing the doorsteps of the garrison church.

"Now yer've spiled it all, sir. I was just a-thinkin' we was 'oldin' our 'ead a trifle too 'igh," said Corporal Stickler, in tones of the deepest remorse at not having spoken sooner and averted the downfall;

and so upset was he by the occurrence, that it was only by standing at the door and administering a smart tap with his pace-stick to each recruit as he filed in that he was able to bring himself into a proper frame of mind for his devotions.

There was a good deal of looking round and tittering amongst the officers as Verisopht took his seat, and it was some time before he was sufficiently composed to look about him and see what sort of a place he was in.

Presbyterian the first thing in the morning, Roman Catholic later on, and now Protestant, the building had in turn been made to do duty as a place of worship for each sect; and even as Verisopht looked on, a few orderlies were removing certain vessels and ornaments used in the Romish ritual.

The sound of a band trumpeting and drumming right up to the church-door now diverted Verisopht's attention, and another regiment trooped in to the strains of "We'll run 'em in," and, after a good deal of clatter and unclasping of waist-belts, settled down. Then another band clashed and clanged, and another regiment poured in, until the whole building was full of a bright mass of uniforms.

It was all a very novel sight to Verisopht; but still more novel was it to see a staff officer in uniform, with medals on his breast and his sword girded about him, reading the lessons; and reading them right well, too, and just as devoutly and impressively as if he had been a mitred bishop in lawn sleeves.

This impressed Verisopht very much, and, as he noticed how quietly and attentively the men listened, he could not help wishing that Aunt Millicent could witness the whole scene, and then perhaps she would not have such a dreadful opinion of soldiers; in fact, Verisopht thought he had never seen a congregation where there was so little turning about of heads and whispering as in the present one of great, rough, burly men, concerning whom many people share Aunt Millicent's opinions.

The service was rather a short one, and after the military chaplain had concluded a homely and simple discourse to suit his hearers, the regiment marched back to quarters.

Amongst the officers at the camp, Sunday was a great day for long walks in the country, and after lunch Verisopht joined a large party and spent the afternoon amongst the green Hampshire lanes and fields in the vicinity of the camp. After dinner he retired at an early hour to his quarters, and occupied himself up to bedtime in writing a long letter home; so that, altogether, Verisopht spent his first Sunday in that den of iniquity, a soldier's barrack, in a way with which even Aunt Millicent could have found but little fault.

CHAPTER XV.

Our hero serves his country with energy and zeal—
He sees much of that great man Corporal Stickler,
and the more he sees the deeper he is impressed—
He is eager in the pursuit of professional knowledge
—He passes triumphantly through at a trying ordeal
and treads the stony path of duty—He obtains
"leave of absence on private affairs" and previous
to his departure, obeys an injunction touching the
moral welfare of the benighted soldier.

VERISOPHT'S life for the next few weeks was one continued round of drill. Before breakfast, between breakfast and lunch, between lunch and dinner, at all hours of the day, he was to be seen, in company of Corporal Stickler and a squad of recruits, in sundry graceful and soldier-like attitudes. Sometimes his arms were extended after the fashion of a sign-post, or whirling wildly round him like a windmill in a hurricane. At other times he might be seen vainly struggling to bring his fingers and toes into contact without bending his knees; and the energy and zeal with which he served his country at this period no one could have testified to more strongly than his servant, on whom devolved the duty of replacing the buttons and braces carried away in action.

Then, too, it was a stirring sight, and one which would have kindled a glow of pride in the family bosom, to see him heading a long string of recruits in a graceful and domestic-birdlike movement termed, properly, the "balance," irreverently, the "goose step."

There was not the monotony about these drills which might be supposed. For instance, what could be more exciting than when the string of recruits on being told to turn in one direction immediately, on a *tot homines quot sententiæ* principle, turned outwards in several? What, indeed, except perhaps when it turned inwards, and the two inner men, their noses almost flattened to their faces by the concussion, were kept marking time, with the injured features one inch apart, while Corporal Stickler, bristling as to his moustache, and charged with vituperation to the very tuft on his forage-cap, was bearing down upon them from the centre of the square, not exactly on the wings of love.

Though Verisopht was very often the cause of these little variations, the effect never fell directly upon him. Corporal Stickler could not with propriety pour out the vials of his wrath on his officer's head, but, by a tacit and an instinctive understanding between the two, he had a way of reaching him through a particularly mild little recruit who rarely went wrong. For instance, when Corporal Stickler would say "To the r-r-right tur-r-run!" and Verisopht with characteristic presence of mind would promptly branch off to the left; or when at the order, "Left whe-e-el!" he would instantly start off to the right on a solitary and vague march across the square, Corporal Stickler would swoop down on the small recruit, who had acted up to the very letter of the mandate, and, after applying the torture of the moustache, as previously explained, would burst forth into invective: "Aha! set the orficer wrong, did yer, e-h-h? Yer'll be shot for insubordination afore yer've done solgering —*I* see. Didn't understand the word o' command, eh? Blessed if yer don't look like a monkey when he ain't quite sure where the flea's a-bitin' of 'im. Stand still, can't you, e-eh?" (This probably when the small recruit dared to wink his eyes.) "If you was more like a man and less like a flamingo darncin' a 'ornpipe we might make somethink of yer."

Corporal Stickler's detractors were wont to hold that these shafts of sarcasm were the result of laboured composition rather than the spontaneous outburst of innate wit. But, whether they were right or wrong, Corporal Stickler's similes and figures of speech seldom failed him under about ten minutes' fling, and then he would shake the wretched little recruit until his forage-cap, always several sizes too big for him, would get well shaken over his eyes, in which condition it was not long before he committed himself on his own account, and received another dressing accordingly.

Verisopht used to feel very much for the little recruit, and once after a drill he surreptitiously presented him with half a sovereign. This the recruit was graciously pleased to accept, and the following morning the whole squad were had up before the Colonel charged with drunkenness. Verisopht was at a loss to account for this sudden and wholesale backsliding, and was, luckily, in the innocence of his heart, spared the painful reflection that he himself had been the cause of it all.

At this period it may be said that Corporal Stickler was the guiding-star of Verisopht's existence, and consequently I dwell on his portrait longer than I should otherwise do. Personality was Corporal Stickler's principal weapon of speech, and he wielded it unsparingly. To a man whose nose happened to be, poetically speaking, somewhat "tiptilted" he would sometimes say, "Now then; when you've done scratchin' the top o' yer 'ead with that ther' elephant's trunk o' yourn we'll get on a bit better p'r'aps." At other times he would remark to the same individual, "If you don't like the regiment, say so; but don't go and always be a-turnin' yer nose up at the number of it on yer forage-cap in that there outrigeous manner!"

Occasionally he would strike still deeper. To some wretched, homesick little recruit he would roar out, "Now then, what's number three from the right a-thinkin' of? *I* know. He's a-thinkin' of his 'appy 'ome. But what I tells number three from the right is this 'ere.—He won't see his 'appy 'ome no more."

Having by this dismal prophecy reduced number three from the right to a state of abject despair, in which he very soon committed some fresh blunder, Corporal Stickler would go at him again with, "What! a-thinkin' o' that ther' 'appy 'ome agin, are yer, what you ain't agoin' to see no more? We'll make a 'appy 'ome for yer! Such a 'appy 'ome that bless'd if it won't be like a little 'olliday to yer to go and 'ave a tooth drawed."

I do not think that Corporal Stickler had really a very hard heart, but he had a hard theory that if you spared a recruit's feelings you spoiled a good soldier; and, to do him justice, I must say that, whatever his faults might have been, there never was a drill instructor who so speedily transformed a slovenly young clod or an insubordinate young cockney into a smart, obedient soldier as he did.

So much of Verisopht's thoughts and time did Corporal Stickler, at this period, absorb, that our hero had but few opportunities during the day of mixing with his brother-officers. At nights, however, he occasionally saw a little more of them than was quite pleasant; for it would frequently happen that after he had retired to bed he would be aroused out of his slumbers by a most fearful din, to find anything, from a bulldog to a donkey, in his bed; while around was a group of tormenting demons in the shape of noisy young subalterns. It was no use locking his door. In the first place, the Royal Engineers, with true *esprit de corps*, had made the bolt shoot the wrong way; in the second, when he had had this slight error of judgment remedied, he found that, like Love, these boisterous spirits of the night "laughed at locksmiths." He had begun by standing on his dignity; but this had always ended in his finding himself sitting in the cold tub, placed overnight ready for the morrow's ablutions, or being buried alive under the weight of his own furniture, which these fiends would pile up on top of his bed, where he lay. If, on the other hand, he received his unwelcome visitors with a tolerable show of politeness, they abstained from laying violent hands on him, and would content themselves with calling for his song, "Then let me like a soldier fall." The shortest way out of the difficulty was generally to sit up in bed at once and do what they wished. By this course Verisopht soon enjoyed an almost complete immunity from these visits.

So eager was Verisopht in the pursuit of professional knowledge that, not content with the practical tuition of Corporal Stickler, he would follow up the subject theoretically in his own room, with the aid of his drill-book and numerous little blocks of coloured wood to represent soldiers. To these he would issue the words of command in a loud tone of voice, and then move them into their proper places; and by this means Mentor, who was a quick bird, was soon able to intersperse his moral precepts with a fair amount of drill, and became, conversationally, a cross between Mr. Chadband and Corporal Stickler.

Sometimes Captain Calipash or Captain Chutney would drop in and proffer their assistance; but when they did, the business on hand soon wandered off to the West or East Indies. Captain Calipash generally had the MS. of his poem, "The Land of the Guava and Turtle," contributed to the "Tobago Tickler," in his pocket; and he rarely paid a visit without treating Verisopht to a reading, always prefacing the same with "I don't think you have heard this before, Boomershine;" and Verisopht was a great deal too polite and considerate to contradict him, although he knew every word from beginning to end. Equally by heart did he soon know every one of Captain Chutney's Indian adventures; but the same politeness and consideration shown to Captain Calipash was extended to his rival Captain Chutney, and he would listen with apparent interest to each adventure up to the crowning-point, when the phrase, "I pledge you my sacred word of honour, sir, as an officer and a gentleman," ushered in the highest-coloured point of the narrative.

Altogether, there was a sameness in the visits of Captains Chutney and Calipash, except when they happened simultaneously, and then there was always an exciting passage of arms between the two.

Wilder would also occasionally break in upon the young soldier's studies, and tender his assistance; but mystification and wonder, rather than enlightenment, attended his explanations.

In spite, however, of all such drawbacks, Verisopht stuck diligently to his drill-book and blocks of wood; and before two months of soldiering had passed over his head he was considered by Corporal Stickler, the sergeant-major, and the Adjutant (the triumvirate which up to now had guided his destinies) in a fit state to go before the commanding officer for final examination previous to being "dismissed drill." This ordeal may be termed the "little go" of a military career; and it was with a fearful sense of its importance that Verisopht presented himself on the barrack square before the Colonel to undergo it. Luckily, nothing could exceed the good-humour and urbanity of the chief, who had just gained another victory over the War Office—this time over a disputed two shillings and eightpence three farthings—and Verisopht came off with flying colours.

"And now," said the Colonel, "as you have been very attentive and diligent, you may have a fortnight's leave as soon as you have done a supernumerary garrison guard and a regimental duty. Put him on as supernumerary, Mr. Dressop," continued the Colonel to the Adjutant, "with the officer on regimental duty to-morrow, and with the subaltern on guard the next time we furnish the garrison duties."

Verisopht was very proud of having acquitted himself so well, and Corporal Stickler received a handsome reward for all his care and attention.

As he was dressing for mess in the evening, the orderly corporal of his company came in with the "orders."

"Anything particular in orders, corporal?" asked Verisopht, who was anxious to hear his own name mentioned for duty.

"Yes, sir. Mr. Wilder, 'e's for regimental duty, and you're stupidnumery, sir."

"Thank you," said Verisopht, with an inward wish that the corporal would be a little more particular in his pronunciation.

Verisopht's duty the next day consisted in following Wilder about at intervals from seven o'clock in the morning to ten o'clock at night; and if he did not learn much, the fault could not be laid on his mentor's want of imagination.

A few days afterwards he found himself as supernumerary on guard with the same individual; and after twenty-four hours of it he came off this duty with a hazy idea that it consisted mainly in dispensing sherry and brandy-and-soda, throughout the day and the greater part of the night, to a rapid succession of visitors from different parts of the camp.

Far be it from the writer to convey the idea that the British officer performs his duties carelessly. He is as strict and conscientious as any officer in the world. Verisopht's notion was owing more to

Hooky Wilder's wondrous popularity throughout the camp than to any slackness and want of zeal on the part of that young officer. In reality no officer in the regiment performed his duty better than Wilder, but he had a way of doing it and letting it alone afterwards. The men idolised him. On a long march under burning suns when the hard shakos galled the throbbing temples, and the tightly-braced knapsack straps confined the heart thumping loudly for more room, and the regiment lagged and trailed wearily along, there was always one company which marched with jaunty step and cheerful mien, and that was Hooky Wilder's.

Of all officers in the regiment the one to lead a Forlorn Hope would have been Hooky Wilder. The men would have followed him anywhere, and his lead would have taken them to Death or Glory.

So far Verisopht Boomershine had acquitted himself well, and I must not forget to add that whereas any attempt to smoke a cigar had at first invariably been followed by a hasty and unsteady exit from the company, he could now perform the feat, and did so after dinner on guest-nights without any more serious results than a trifling clamminess about the forehead and a slight coldness down the back, which would soon wear off; so that his improvement on this point was most marked. To be sure, he had not yet learned to swear at his servant, but he had once been heard to say in his absence, "Drat him!" which, at any rate, was a step in the right direction.

Having thus acquired the rudiments of a military education, it was with a proud sense of his increased importance that he prepared to avail himself of Colonel Rooteen's kind offer of three weeks' "leave of absence on private affairs."

At the very first prospect of a return to the family bosom, he had sent Mentor to the men's rooms, in deference to the wishes of the donor that he might occasionally be hung up amongst the "soldiers, poor benighted ones," with the view of mending their morals by his admonitions and precepts. With this object the virtuous bird was left behind,

CHAPTER XVI.

Is so shocking that people of weak nerves are recommended to let it alone—Mentor becomes a painful instance of the truth of his own favourite precept—Wholesale slander—Virtuous indignation—Ingenious scheme for the regeneration of Africa—A shadow darkens the once hopeful House of Boomershine.

GREAT was the rejoicing in the House of Boomershine over the soldier's return. Carry and Fanny were for having quite a ceremonious reception, and talked of greeting his arrival with "See, the conquering hero comes," on the piano; but Mr. Boomershine, with considerable truth and humour, remarked that probably the only thing he had conquered during his absence had been his aversion to smoking, and that, as this was such a common event amongst young men, it was hardly worth making a fuss about.

On the day he was expected Verisopht had not been able to get away from Aldershot until after parade, and consequently it was not until the evening that he stood once more under the roof of his forefathers. It was unanimously pronounced that he had improved very much in figure and appearance, and that he had quite a military air about him; though Mrs. Boomershine in her heart was just a little disappointed that he had not grown six inches in the two months he had been away, as she had always been led to believe that drill had such a wonderful effect upon the growth of youth; and Carry and Fanny were also a little disappointed to find that his moustache was still, as when he left them, barely discernible to the naked eye. These trifles, however, were of momentary consideration, and what he had failed to gain in stature and moustache was more than atoned for by his martial bearing; for

Verisopht evidently considered it due to the honour of the cloth, as its only representative down in those parts, to be so hyper-military in his carriage that he always looked in danger of tumbling over backwards.

The three weeks' leave passed quickly and pleasantly. The whole family vied with each other in making a hero of him, and Verisopht in return enlivened them with many anecdotes about Wilder and his brother-officers, as also with some extracts from the thrilling adventures of Captains Calipash and Chutney in the West and East Indies respectively.

The only alloy in our hero's enjoyment was the unaccountable and extremely trying behaviour of the maids. The first report of his coming had thrown them into a state of pleasurable excitement, owing to a belief that it was the invariable custom of a red-coat to kiss every pretty girl that crossed his path, and that Verisopht, true to the traditions of his class, would of course adopt this playful way they had in the army. In this expectation they adorned themselves with their prettiest ribands, and whenever they met him on the stairs there would be a great deal of giggling and simpering, and a glance or two, as much as to say, " Oh, you wicked thing, you !" And then they would rush away, as if in such dreadfully dangerous proximity their characters were at stake. This was all fearfully embarrassing to poor Verisopht—so much so that, after the first two or three days, whenever he had occasion to go upstairs or downstairs, he would try, under some excuse, to obtain one of his sisters as a convoy, and, failing this, would previously reconnoitre to see if the coast were clear, and then make a bolt for it as if ten thousand Bashi-Bazouks were at his heels. By this course he brought much contempt and obloquy upon himself, and the maids, as they hauled down their pennons and streamers, agreed amongst themselves with considerable disgust that " Mr. Verisopht was quite unfit for the harmy, and didn't ought to be in it."

Of course Aunt Millicent had not been left in ignorance of so important a family event as the return of the young warrior, and two days before the expiration of his leave Mr. Boomershine received a letter from her, announcing her intention of paying them all a visit that very day, with the double purpose of again beholding the dear bird Mentor, and of judging for herself to what extent Verisopht's morals had as yet been corrupted by his military experience.

"Dear me, Verry," said Mr. Boomershine, "you have not brought Mentor."

"No," replied Verisopht; "Aunt Millicent said, you know, he was to be hung up amongst the men occasionally, and when I came away I thought it would be a good opportunity to do so, and left him with them."

"Well, telegraph for him to be brought at once by special messenger," said Mr. Boomershine. "It will never do to disappoint Aunt Millicent; the consequences might be serious."

To avert such a calamity Verisopht telegraphed as directed, and in the course of the afternoon Aunt Millicent arrived accompanied by a few of her favourite pets. She was a spare old lady in old-fashioned garb and of abrupt manners. Her eyes were very nearly colourless, and in her countenance there was a rigidity which rarely relaxed except when the colourless eyes rested on a parrot, a tabby, or a plethoric little dog of her own rearing, and then her face would light up with considerable animation.

The rigid countenance became more rigid still when she found that Mentor was not present to welcome her with a moral precept; but she became reconciled to his absence when Verisopht explained that he had been, according to her own injunctions, left with the soldiers, and that he had been telegraphed for and would arrive late in the day.

Aunt Millicent's visits were not exactly of a jubilant nature. The family was on its best behaviour; and there are few more uncomfortable conditions of mind and body than this. The children went about with scared faces and noiseless steps, and the only creature who seemed to enjoy any liberty of action was the wretched little dog that came up with her. As soon as she had settled down she commenced making herself agreeable by hearing the younger children their catechisms all round, and then read Carry, Fanny, and Verisopht a lecture on the follies and vanities of this life, occasionally disconcerting Mr. Boomershine himself with a vicious backhander, as he stood by enjoining his children to lay to heart all that Aunt Millicent was telling them.

Luckily for Carry and Fanny, just as Aunt Millicent had only arrived at the sixth head of her discourse, the announcement of dinner put an end to their torture.

The meal was by no means a lively one. Even the generally irrepressible Peter, who was the youngest at the table, was silent on the subject of his progress in Latin; and depressing periods of stillness were constantly exercising their icy influence over the scene.

With the dessert, a string of small Boomershines, brushed and frilled and headed by the twins hand-in-hand, made its appearance. It really seemed, though, as if nothing could go off well under Aunt Millicent's auspices. The procession had been most carefully marshalled outside by the two nursemaids, but owing to its keeping its eyes fixed on Aunt Millicent, instead of on its course, it speedily fell into disorder. First of all the twins tumbled over each other, and then the remainder of the procession tumbled over the twins.

"I never saw such stupid, awkward children as yours, Caroline," said Aunt Millicent, as the little Boomershines, scared more than ever out of their senses, picked themselves up, and, still keeping their eyes fixed on their awful relative, climbed into the high chairs placed for them at the table.

Mrs. Boomershine's motherly heart swelled, and she was on the point of retorting; but Mr. Boomershine's imploring glances from the head of the table, and consideration for her children's future, restrained her.

"Mentor should be here by this time," said Mr. Boomershine, by way of leading the conversation into a channel agreeable to Aunt Millicent.

"Talk of the——"

"Ahem—'an angel,' Carry, my dear, 'and you see the wings,'" said Mr. Boomershine, saving, with wonderful presence of mind, his eldest daughter from a terrible *faux pas*, as a servant entered with Mentor.

Aunt Millicent jumped up with an exclamation of delight, and hung fondly over the cage.

Whatever are a soldier's faults, unkindness to animals is assuredly not one of them, and Mentor was looking in first-rate condition, and had evidently been well cared for. He seemed, however, a little strange, the result of travel, probably, and abstained from making any remarks.

Aunt Millicent gazed fondly upon him, and then proceeded, almost with tears in her eyes, to improve the occasion as the family crowded round.

"It is impossible," said Aunt Millicent, "to look upon him without being deeply moved, when one thinks of how, for the last fortnight, he has been using those accomplishments which I taught him for the purpose of softening the hard hearts of those sinful soldiers, 'Evil,'" said Aunt Millicent, bending over Mentor and prompting him to the utterance of his favourite precept. "'Evil.'"

Mentor cocked his head on one side with intense earnestness, as if saying, "That strikes familiarly on my ears. Be good enough to repeat it."

"'Evil,'" said Aunt Millicent, in coaxing tones.

"Once more, please. I don't think you're quite right," Mentor seemed to say with an extra cock of his head.

"'Evil,'" repeated Aunt Millicent.

"Devil," said Mentor triumphantly, as if he had at last got hold of it; "devil take the hindmost! Devil a bit! Go to the devil!"

Aunt Millicent started back as if she had been stung by a cobra-di-capello, which we believe to be the deadliest of the serpent tribe.

"Go to the devil and shake yourself!" said Mentor, getting more abusive, step by step; and having now got thoroughly at home with his subject, he applied with great volubility some fearfully opprobrious epithets to the surrounding company.

Such abominable use did he make of his vile little black tongue, that "at every word a reputation died." At one fell swoop he took Mrs. Boomershine's character away and cast it to the winds. He threw horrible doubts on the legitimacy of all the young Boomershines. At Miss Millicent Simple, his virtuous, his kind preceptor, he hurled what may be termed a colloquial brick-bat which felled her to the nearest sofa. Finally, against Mr. Boomershine he brought an accusation under which that fine old English gentleman fairly staggered.

The consternation was terrible. Mrs. Boomershine snatched some of her innocent offspring to her bosom, and rushed away with them; Aunt Millicent nearly fainted; and Mr. Boomershine laid virtuously indignant hands on the cage and bore Mentor out of the room, the depraved bird cursing deeply the whole time, and reiterating the fearful charges he had brought against nearly all those present.

* * * * *

Half an hour afterwards Aunt Millicent shook the dust off her feet, as she departed from the home of the Boomershines. A fly was in readiness to carry her to the railway, and in her hand, as she strode down the doorsteps regardless of all family attempts at pacification, was what looked like a huge bundle of wraps. It was Mentor, muffled in a flannel petticoat, a blanket, and a railway rug. But nothing could stifle his tones, and his muffled curses were the last sounds the Boomershines heard as their outraged relative, without so much as a farewell glance, stepped into the fly and drove away.

The next day Verisopht received the following :—

"Dear Verisopht,

"I little thought that Mentor (or rather '*Tor*mentor,' as he will be called until regenerated) would ever be so terrible an instance of what used to be his favourite precept, that 'Evil communications corrupt good manners.' That he is so, he affords painful proof every moment of the day; for, alas! his language continues fearful; so much so that I have ordered all the maid-servants to stuff cotton wool into their ears. On you, who went into the army against my advice, and on your parents, who allowed you to take the fatal step, I lay all the blame. It is therefore right that you should suffer. I mean to establish forthwith a Reformatory Home, on an enormous scale, for Soldiers' and

Sailors' Parrots. Besides reformation, the following is the noble work which this Institution will accomplish. These birds will be collected by hundreds, and when their minds are well stored with moral precepts they will be shipped off, each bird being provided with a small white tie round its neck, to Africa, and there let loose amongst their feathered brethren. These, in their turn, will soon acquire these precepts, and impart them to others of their species. In this way the whole of that now heathenish land, from north to south, from east to west, will positively teem with virtuous admonition. The very air will be charged with principles of rectitude, and in an atmosphere of such moral purity it will be impossible for the most hardened native to continue in his wicked ways. All the money I had intended leaving you, or any of your family, I shall bequeath to this noble institution. I have nothing more to add, except that I have done with you all.

"Your shocked and outraged aunt,
"MILLICENT SIMPLE."

So here was an end to all the great expectations from Aunt Millicent. Truly, Verisopht's leave had a sorrowful ending, and he returned to his regiment, leaving his once hopeful home under a gloomy cloud of disappointment.

CHAPTER XVII.

Return to Duty—Verisopht becomes an authority—Change of quarters—Sensation in Snoozleton—Different views of the British soldier—Aunt Millicent flees from contamination.

"HOLLOA, Boomershine! how did you enjoy yourself?" said Wilder, bursting into our hero's quarters, as he was hurriedly dressing himself for mess after his return journey. "I saw a light in your room, and concluded you had come back. What have you done with old 'Evil communications?'"

"What, Mentor?"

"Yes."

"He'll never come back," replied Verisopht ruefully. "When I was away he was in the barrack-room, and the men taught him some fearful language. He swore most horribly at my aunt, who gave him to me, and she's taken him away, and cut me off with a shilling."

Instead of Wilder being shocked or showing any sympathy, he declared, between shouts of laughter, that it was the best thing he had heard for some time, and that Verisopht would be the death of him some day.

"By-the-way," he said, as soon as he had recovered a little, "I've some news for you. You're a Snoozleshire man, aren't you?"

"Yes."

"Well, we're under orders for that part of the world, and we'll most likely be off in a fortnight. They're going to make a military station of Snoozleton, and are doing up the old militia barracks for us. There hasn't been a regiment there for about forty years, and we'll just jerk them up a bit."

"Snoozleton!" said Verisopht; "why,

that's my aunt's post-town, and it's about twelve miles from our place."

Here the mess-bugle sounded, and Wilder, who was dressed for dinner, departed.

"I'll tell old Calipash and Chutney you're coming. They've been so hard up for a listener since you've been away, that, by Jove! they've been nearly driven to telling their yarns to each other."

Verisopht hurriedly completed his toilet and followed to the mess-room, where the repast had already begun. Wilder was setting the whole table in a roar, and Verisopht, as he took his seat, was painfully conscious that he and Mentor were the subjects of amusement. Even Captain Calipash, who never laughed at any stories but his own, said it was "Capital, and reminded him of something which once occurred to his poor friend Calipee, in the West Indies, when——"

Here groans from all parts of the table nipped the West Indian reminiscence in the bud.

"The way in which Captain Calipash's story has been met," said Captain Chutney, with an ill-disguised air of triumph, "puts me in mind of a scene I once witnessed in India. By gad! it was the most extraordinary——"

Here the East Indian anecdote met the same fate as the West Indian, and Captain Calipash, in his turn, looked triumphant. After this the two rival heroes of romance confined their attentions to Verisopht. Their polite listener's ears, however, were not entirely at their service. He was in very general request throughout the whole of the evening. Every one, in view of the approaching move of the regiment, had something to ask him about Snoozleshire. Were the girls pretty? Were there any heiresses to be picked up? What sort of hunting and shooting was there? Were people inclined to be civil and hospitable? and a host of other questions, which Verisopht answered to the best of his ability.

It was not only for this evening, but during the remainder of the time before the move, that Verisopht found himself in the pleasant and flattering position of an oracle consulted by his brother-officers on every conceivable subject in connection with their new quarters. Major and Brevet Lieutenant-Colonel Quiverful, who had two marriageable daughters on his hands, took him on one side and asked him confidentially whether there were any nice young men of property about Snoozleton; Captain Spott-Browne, the great billiard-player, who, like the fish in the poem, " sucked in his prey at his favourite pool," was particularly anxious to know if there was a county club in Snoozleton, with a good billiard-table, where a friendly game of pool might be got up in the afternoons; Lieutenant Slowcock, the Staff College candidate, whether he knew of a clergyman who would read mathematics with him; Lieutenant Spavin, whether he thought it would be a good place to sell a screw; Captain Thruster, whether it was a grass country, or plough, or what, and what the fences were like; Captain Calipash, whether he didn't think, if only that consummate old fool Chutney could be kept out of the way, a series of lectures on the West Indies, in the Working Men's Institute, would be a pleasing novelty to the bucolic mind down there; Captain Chutney, if he didn't think the same on India would be acceptable, if only that confounded old ass Calipash could be prevented from shoving in his oar with his sickening West Indies, &c., &c.

The thirst for information was not confined to Verisopht's brother-officers. The news that the regiment was going to Snoozleton created intense excitement in the Boomershine family. Mr. and Mrs. Boomershine became suddenly solicitous concerning the prospects and expectations of the young officers; and Carry and Fanny wanted to know if there wouldn't be a great deal of theatricals and balls and picnics going on directly they arrived.

The approaching move soon plunged the regiment into discomfort and apparent confusion. The mess was broken up, officers' baggage packed, and all the goods and

HE WOULD BE A SOLDIER!

chattels were piled up on the barrack square, to be carted away to the station by the Army Service Corps. The officers were, of course, honorary members of the mess of the regiment in the next lines, and had their meals there; but a strange mess is like a strange club, never as comfortable as your own, and there was a great deal of sitting about disconsolately on the piles of baggage, and longing to get away and settle down in the new quarters.

The wished-for day at last arrived, and the 119th, headed by the different bands of the brigade, marched down to the railway station at an early hour. In the afternoon they arrived at Snoozleton, which was quite in a state of excitement at the novel sight of a regiment marching up its main street, band playing and colours flying.

The advent of the gallant 119th was viewed with mingled feelings in Snoozleton. The young damsels of the counter and the regions below stairs were unanimous in their approval of the warriors; but the youth of the town, who had hitherto had it all their own way in the evenings and on Saturday and Sunday afternoons, said " *they* didn't want no soldiers comin' gallavantin' about." The butcher who had obtained the contract for supplying the regiment with meat remarked to the baker who had been similarly fortunate regarding his stock-in-trade, that " the British army was a glorious institootion," and that " the sight of a red-coat ought to make the heart of a true Briton throb in his breeches-pocket "—he begged the baker's pardon, he meant " bosom." He kept his note-book in the former, and as he was fingering it at the time, the confusion of ideas was natural. To this the lucky baker assented in quite a glow of patriotism ; but the other bakers and butchers, who had tried hard to get the contracts and had failed, agreed that " soldiers was the scum of the earth, and had ought to be put down." Another party in and about Snoozleton turned up its eyes and asked what was to become of the Snoozleton morals. The bitterest in this lot was Aunt Millicent. "What, live within a couple of miles of a regiment of soldiers? Not she! She would sooner die!" And so, closing up her house and putting it in the hands of an agent, she fled, bag and baggage, from the contaminated atmosphere to a purer and more remote corner of the county.

CHAPTER XVIII.

A distinguished veteran—A sop to Cerberus—The light fantastic toe—Our special correspondents—Eccentricities of matured military genius.

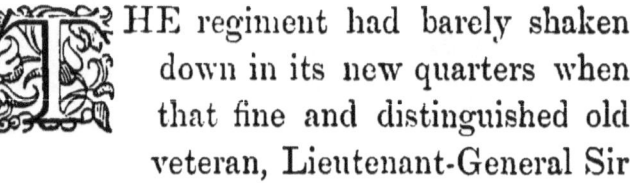HE regiment had barely shaken down in its new quarters when that fine and distinguished old veteran, Lieutenant-General Sir Charles Colley-Whobble, K.C.B., the commander of the district, announced his intention of paying it a visit of inspection. On this it was at once determined to give a ball, which would afford the new-comers an opportunity of making the acquaintance of the surrounding people, and would also be a sop to the old General not to snarl

and be unpleasant. To most old gentlemen the prospect of a ball would have been anything but mollifying; but Sir Charles Colley-Whobble had retained a weakness for gaiety and society ever since the days when, as bewitching Captain Colley (he came into the Whobble estates afterwards), he had danced and flirted as became a gay young *militaire*. He also had other weaknesses, had Sir Charles Colley-Whobble; but it is only due to him to add that his language, when under excitement, was not open to this reproach.

The festive intentions were soon noised abroad, much to the delight of the giddy youth of the vicinity, and the dejection of the papas and mammas, to most of whom a ball was only another term for half-a-dozen hours of penance in an uncomfortable dress in the dead of night.

The cards of invitation threw many a quiet country home into a flutter of excitement, and drove many a fair young damsel beside herself with the momentous consideration of what she should wear. But in all Snoozleshire no two young hearts fluttered more wildly than those of Carry and Fanny Boomershine. It was to be their first ball. The interval between the receipt of the invitation and the momentous evening was spent in exciting preparations. A great deal of time was devoted to practising the *trois temps* with each other; and sometimes even their brother Peter, who had about as much idea of waltzing as he had of ballooning, was pressed into the service. At first Mrs. Boomershine played the "Copenhagen Waltzes" for them; but Carry and Fanny turned up their noses at the old familiar tune, and insisted on their mother learning the "Blue Danube" or the "Manolo" instead.

Having said this much about the ball, it might be tantalising to our fair young readers not to say more; and, out of deference to their possible wishes on the subject, we transcribe the following correspondence :—

No. 1.

From Miss Fanny Boomershine to her "bosom friend Katie," not yet emancipated from the thraldom of Miss MacTurk, Brighton.

"My darling Katie,

"I've such a lot to tell you, I hardly know how to begin. First of all, you know, I promised you faithfully I'd write and tell you all about my first ball, and now I'm going to keep my promise. *It's over! I've been to one!* Oh, such a delightful ball, darling! I wish you could have been there. It was given by my brother Verry's regiment, which is quartered at Snoozleton, about twelve miles off, and has only just come here. Some of the dresses were lovely, but I'll only give you a description of mine; and mind you let me know what you think of it. It was a white *poult-de-soie* with a tunic of white *gaze de chamberry*, trimmed with darling little quillings of *tulle*, and looped up with lilies of the valley; and then in my hair I had a long spray of lilies of the valley. It looked sweet, *I* think; but let me know how *you* like it. Carry was dressed just in the same way. We posted over from here, and as we got near the barracks, where the ball was to be, I began to feel awfully nervous, and I could hear Carry's teeth chattering and feel her leg trembling against mine, although it wasn't a bit cold. As we drove up to the entrance it looked like a glimpse into fairyland. There was such an array of flags and glitter of uniforms, and stars made of flashing swords, it nearly took my breath away; and there, ready to receive the guests, were a lot of officers so polite and nice; and I felt so proud to see Verry in his regimentals amongst them. I wish he'd give up blushing, though. It's so unsoldierlike. I felt my heart right up in my mouth just like when Miss MacTurk caught us reading 'The Mysterious Stranger' in school hours, and you told such a horrid tarradiddle and said it was one of Miss Edgeworth's tales—don't you recollect? Well,

I never felt so nervous in all my life, and my hand trembled so when I put it into the arm of my first partner that I felt quite ashamed; but it all wore off after I had been in the room ten minutes, and then I *did* enjoy myself so. I declare I won't marry any one but an officer. I couldn't help thinking what a noble profession the army is, and what a glorious thing it must be to feel oneself enrolled as one of the defenders of our country. I felt that I would have given anything to be a man, and I'm certain I wouldn't in the least mind marching up to the cannon's mouth, if I was quite sure there was nothing in it and the band would only keep playing one of those lovely German waltzes all the time. There is something so romantic about it all. An old General was there, darling, who had been inspecting, I think they call it, the regiment that day. Such a gallant veteran he was, covered with medals; and when he walked about he made such a chinking that, if you had shut your eyes as he passed, you would almost have thought you were in church with a collection for indigent Hindoos going on. I can fancy the devotion all the officers and men must feel towards him, and how they must all long for the time for him to lead them to victory or death. I could picture him to myself, so vividly, dashing up a breach, sword in hand, cheering on his regiments, and the enemy falling back like waves of the sea. He wasn't a bit stuck-up though, and I saw him putting some half-sovereigns papa had lost to him at whist so good-humouredly into his pocket. Then after supper he was so chatty and full of fun, and actually tried to dance a round dance; but, owing to his wounds, I believe, he was a little unsteady. I had lots of partners. I danced with two such wonderful men—Captain Calipash and Captain Chutney; such travellers they were, and such thrilling adventures they have gone through! It just shows what an out-of-the-way part of the world Snoozleshire is, and what a secluded life we must have led, never to have heard of them until Verry joined; for I'm sure the country must have rung with their exploits, of which there can be no doubt whatever, for I had the accounts from their *own* lips. What an endless source of information and interest they must be to their regiment, and how their brother officers must revel in their tales! With two such men *ennui* must be an impossibility. Oh! but, Katie, the one I liked most was a Mr. Wilder—Reginald Carrington Wilder! Isn't it a lovely name? I looked it out in the Army List. I danced with him four times; and I saw mamma questioning Verry about him at last. Oh, Katie, if she could have heard half the sweet things he said to me! At the top of the room the colours of the regiment were crossed— the flags, darling, they rally round and wave to encourage the soldiers in battle. I could picture him, so well, gallantly defending them from the grasp of the enemy, and then, when he could fight no longer— perhaps lost an arm or a leg—wrapping himself up in them and dying sweetly and nobly on the battle-field, with an upturned countenance, and a message and a lock of hair to his mother, cut off by a wounded comrade, gallantly carrying him in under a heavy fire! It's astonishing how easily, when one really *feels* with one's subject, the ideas come without one's exactly knowing how. I have no time for more. Mind you let me know how you liked my dress, and what you think of *him*.

"Your bosom friend,

"Fanny."

No. 2.

From "Katie," at Miss MacTurk's Seminary, Brighton, to her "bosom friend Fanny."

"My darling Fanny,

"It must have been heavenly! I can only write a few lines. Miss MacTurk thinks this is a French exercise I'm at. I am quite ready to love him, darling, as a brother, for your sake. Your dress was *too* awfully lovely; I read the description over and over again. I quite agree with you.——Excuse the crumple, darling; that old pig, MacTurk, suddenly came in, and I had to put this into my pocket. I was going to say I quite agree with you about the army. It's a noble profession; and they generally have such lovely partings to the backs of their heads. No more at present, from your loving

"KATIE.

"P.S.—You made a mistake, darling. It was *you*, not *I*, told the tarradiddle about the book."

No. 3.

From Lieutenant R. C. Wilder, alias "Hooky," to one "Bob," a friend at Aldershot.

"MY DEAR BOB,

"It's not exactly the witching hour of night, when churchyards yawn, &c.; but it's a precious dead-and-alive sort of a time, and if the churchyards don't yawn *I* do, and enough in that line, too, for Kensal Green, Père la Chaise, Woking Cemetery, and any others you can think of, all put

together. To be a little more explicit, it's
6.30 A.M., and there's not a soul about
except the poor devil of a subaltern on
duty, and that's me. I always get stuck
for duty, somehow, after a hard night. I
reverse the usual order of duty and pleasure.
It's pleasure first and duty afterwards with
me, and I don't find duty any the pleasanter, I can assure you, for being taken in
that order. We gave a hop last night;
and after the womenkind had departed, we
kept the ball rolling until past five, and as
I had to be out on parade at six I didn't
see the fun of turning in; so, disconsolate
and melancholy, I sat in the ante-room,
surveying with a jaundiced, and I'm afraid
bloodshot orb the dispiriting débris of the
previous night's debauch; and I quite
realised that it's not the liveliest thing
going, to

"'Feel like one who treads alone the banquet-hall
deserted,
Whose guests are fled, whose garlands dead, and all
but he departed.'

By-the-way, I suppose Moore, being an

Irishman, called it 'desarted.' I never thought of that before, but perhaps when the liquor is just dying in one I may be a little hypercritical. At last I caught sight of pens, ink, and paper, and by a complicated and ingenious train of thought they suggested writing, and writing put me in mind that I owed you a letter, and as I felt uncommonly chippy I thought it might be refreshing if I paid something I owed just by way of a startling novelty. On this I got a B. and S. from a drowsy waiter just to clear away the cobwebs a bit, and to refer to for ideas as I go on. Now for the latest intelligence. We were inspected yesterday by old Colley-Whobble. Like all these old fossils, he has a hobby, and if you only let him ride it the inspection goes off without a hitch. Old Whobble's hobby is drains. Just let him find out a highly-perfumed drain directly he comes into the barracks, and he'll be in a good humour with himself the whole day, fancying that he, and he only, has saved the regiment from a fearful outbreak of typhoid fever or cholera. The Adjutant of the last regiment he inspected put our Adjutant up to the wrinkle, and now I hand it over to you in case the old boy ever inspects you. He also likes a ball. Just give him a good odorous drain in the morning and a ball in the evening, and he'll swear you're the smartest regiment he ever inspected. But omit either of these little attentions, and you'll probably find yourself soldiering in the West Indies or the coast of Africa before a month's out. We managed it capitally. The pioneers had orders to stir up the drains directly he came in sight; and it was a noble spectacle to see the old warrior sniff the tainted gale as he cantered into the barrack square, surrounded by a brilliant staff with their pocket-handkerchiefs up to their noses. Still more thrilling was it to see the gallant veteran hanging fondly for half an hour over a cesspool, into which all the dead cats and dogs of the neighbourhood had been carefully collected, while the regiment went through its performance to empty benches.

Of course he buttered us up tremendously; and at the ball in the evening he got quite gay and festive, and insisted on dancing, which reminded one of the expiring efforts of a teetotum. There was such a stunning little piece of innocence at the hop last night—all purity, blushes, and lilies of the valley. I've got a bunch of the last in my pocket at the present moment. She is a sister of that refreshing fellow Boomershine, who joined us at Aldershot. I couldn't help launching out rather wildly into the flowery paths of fiction, if it was only just to see her open her big eyes and look so hopelessly astonished, an expression which became her to such an extent that it positively encouraged lying. She was quite refreshing, I assure you, after dodging about all day with old Colley-Whobble, who is made up of equal parts of shop, hair-dye, and drains. I danced with her until I saw the mum anxiously inquiring of her son who I was, and if he didn't say I was heir to a dukedom and fifty thousand a year at the very least, I'll make his life a burthen to him. I wonder if the old governor would come down handsome. If I were a marrying man I might do worse. Here's the orderly corporal come to say 'the rations is ready, and they're a-waitin' for the orficer.' What a change in a few short hours, from lilies of the valley, and pearls dropping from ruby lips, to lumps of raw beef, and 'h's' dropping from the Quartermaster's. But, nevertheless, through all these changing scenes of a subaltern's life,

"Always yours muchly,

"Hooky."

After perusing the foregoing correspondence, the reader will not be surprised to hear that Wilder soon found an opportunity of accompanying his brother subaltern on a visit to the family, and that this speedily led to a visit from the family to the barracks to lunch and be shown the lions. Then after that it was wonderful what a sudden convert to croquet parties and afternoon teas Hooky Wilder became; and whereas formerly he would laugh to scorn all such mild frivolities, he would now think nothing of driving twenty miles for either one or the other. The kindness and consideration, too, he showed Verisopht at this period quite threw into the shade all his previous attentions to his brother subaltern. He would often say, "My dear Boomershine, don't you think you ought to go and see your people to-day? They might be hurt at your neglect; and sooner than allow that I'll drive you over in my dog-cart myself." As Verisopht always reported these noble speeches, it was not to be wondered at that Wilder soon became an object of great popularity and esteem to the family in general, and something rather warmer to a certain member in particular.

CHAPTER XIX.

Is a sad one, inasmuch as the reader bids farewell to three distinguished characters — Climax of the rivalry between Captains Chutney and Calipash— Heartless decree of the Horse Guards—Affecting farewell.

IN the intervals of drill which still occupied a great deal of Verisopht's time, he continued to swallow in about equal doses and with strange infatuation the marvellous adventures and hair-breadth escapes of Captains Chutney and Calipash. Captain Chutney, if he could hit off a moment when Captain Calipash's finger was not hooked in Verisopht's button-hole, would pin him by the ear and bear him off, and Captain Calipash was by no means less assiduous in his attentions.

The ball was not a very remote occurrence when one morning after parade Captain Calipash entered Verisopht's quarters with a mysterious air of subdued jubilation.

" I say, Boomershine, I put it to you as a Snoozleshire man. They seem an intelligent class of people down here. Don't you think a lecture on the West Indies in the Town Hall would go down uncommonly well ?"

Verisopht warmly applauded the design. Captain Calipash looked very pleased and continued :—

" It is not only to the town's-people and working classes that I should address myself; my experience at the ball the other night encourages the idea that the lecture would be acceptable and vastly entertaining to others. A charming family yours, my dear Boomershine. I do not wish to flatter —such a course would be unworthy of both of us. 'He that loves to be flattered is worthy of the flatterer.' I say it in all sincerity — a charming family, my dear fellow, so much soul. I took the liberty of repeating my little effusion about the guava and turtle to your father, and he expressed himself in the highest terms of praise; and your two sisters have solicited copies for their albums. Charming boy, too, that brother of yours, Peter. He undertook to put it into Latin verse for me; but I have had a note from your father this morning—a very nice, kind note indeed, telling me that Peter is worrying himself so over such words as 'guava,' 'sangaree,' 'cassareepe,' and 'pepper-pot,' which cannot be found in any Latin Dictionary, that he fears it will end in brain fever, and begging me to absolve him from his promise, which, of course, I have not hesitated a moment in doing. Ah, if there were only more families like yours in this sceptical unimaginative country we should be a happier people, sir, a happier and a more contented and more poetical people. But let us return to the subject of the lecture. Now the great difficulty will be to get the thing known, and at the same time to keep that insufferable bore Chutney in the dark; for, by gad! sir, such is that man's overweening love of getting people to listen to him, that I verily believe if he obtained an inkling of my project, he'd forestall me with his sickening India and its detestable details about zemindars, and begums, and bandycoots, and puttiwallahs, and all the rest of the abominable jargon. At all risks it must be kept from Chutney until the last moment, and you, as possessing local knowledge and interest, will be just the man to assist me."

Verisopht at once pledged himself to do all in his power. Had Captain Calipash said "just the person" or "just the individual," it is doubtful whether Verisopht would have thrown himself with such zeal into the cause; but "just the man" carried everything before it.

"You know you can be of the greatest service to me, my dear Boomershine, in getting the thing quietly promulgated. You can tell your people, you know, and they'll tell their friends, and *they'll* tell *theirs*, and so on; and with some bills I'll distribute privately amongst the tradespeople and working classes, we'll draw a very good house, I've not the slightest doubt, particularly as no entrance-money will be charged."

Captain Calipash's eyes glistened as he spoke of "a good house," and he was too intoxicated with the delicious prospect to brook much delay.

"The longer it's put off, my dear Boomershine, the greater chance there will be of Chutney finding it out. So I think we had better say next Wednesday, and you'll do all you can to let people know, won't you?"

Verisopht readily undertook this share of the work; and Captain Calipash started off, humming "The land of the guava and turtle" in high glee, to make certain preliminary arrangements.

He had not been gone five minutes

when Captain Chutney made his appearance.

"My dear Boomershine, how that unmitigated West Indian humbug does persecute you! I saw him come here and I have been waiting for the last half hour for him to go, as he is, of all persons in the world, the very last I should like to know anything of what I am going to speak to you about. But first of all you must pledge me your sacred word of honour as an officer and a gentleman, not to breathe a word about it to him."

Verisopht gave the required promise.

"Now, they seem, down in this part of the world, inclined to take kindly to soldiers; and it occurs to me that if I were to give a lecture on India in the Town Hall, it would be a graceful opening to our intercourse with the inhabitants. You, as a man of local experience, will be invaluable to me, and I want your assistance. Of course I may count on that, mayn't I?"

Verisopht blushed and fidgeted about uncomfortably. Was he not already pledged to Captain Calipash? and was not his tongue tied, so that he could not give this as a reason for withholding his services?

Captain Chutney noticed this confusion and hesitation, and his ire rose.

"I suppose, sir, that I'm to understand you refuse?"

"Well, but don't you see?" stammered poor Verisopht.

"Don't I see? Yes, I do see, sir," said Captain Chutney, quite purple in the face. "I see, with both eyes shut, that that insidious sneak, Calipash, has so poisoned your mind with his miserable trash that I look upon you as morally dead—poisoned, poisoned to death, and Calipash is the moral murderer! Good-morning to you, sir," and Captain Chutney bounced out of the room like an ignited rocket.

Verisopht was intensely put out by the occurrence. Hitherto he had listened with equal interest and belief to the stories of Captains Calipash and Chutney; but now the impossibility of serving two masters was exemplified, and the inevitable rupture with one had come. He was on the horns of a dilemma, and in his perplexity he repaired to Wilder for advice.

"Calipash going to give a lecture, is he? and old Chutney on the same tack?" said Wilder, as soon as Verisopht had explained the circumstance to him.

"Yes; don't you see, it's placed me in such an awkward position. I don't want to quarrel with Chutney, he has been very kind to me; and at the same time I must keep my promise to Calipash. What do you advise?"

"My dear fellow, leave old Chutney to me," said Wilder, after a few moments' thought. "I'll manage it all. By-the-way, what evening did you say Calipash's lecture comes off?"

"On Wednesday next. But of course you won't breathe a word of this to Chutney?"

"Not for worlds," replied Wilder in tones which left no doubt of his sincerity.

It was just the very last thing he would have done.

Verisopht was reassured, and departed with a lightened conscience. As he left Wilder's room, he fancied he heard a burst of chuckles, but he thought nothing of it at the moment. Hooky Wilder was addicted to chuckles.

"If my little plan only comes off," soliloquised the treacherous Hooky, "it will be, as Prince Hal said, 'argument for a week, laughter for a month, and a jest for ever.'"

Here bare anticipation was almost too much for him; but he recovered himself, and in five minutes was closeted with Captain Chutney.

As the eventful Wednesday drew near there was about Captain Calipash a hilarious air of anticipation, and a general condition of mind and body known as being "in high feather;" and, strange to say, exactly the same demeanour characterised Captain Chutney at this time; and whenever the two met, each seemed to be laughing in his sleeve. Verisopht noticed, too, that Wilder was a great deal with Captain Chutney, and this was curious, for Wilder was Captain Chutney's most sceptical enemy, and Verisopht had even seen him on occasions when other means had failed, silence his superior officer's flow of narrative with a sofa cushion.

At last the evening arrived, and Verisopht found himself acting as a sort of stage-manager to Captain Calipash. The honour had been gradually thrust on him, somewhat to his embarrassment, but Wilder came forward in the kindest manner possible with his assistance. To be sure, there were certain arrangements which he failed to see the use of; for instance, a baize screen, which was placed down the centre of the stage to within a few feet of the footlights. But when he questioned its utility, Hooky Wilder silenced him with his superior knowledge of stage business.

"It's merely, my dear Boomershine, to take away from the bare effect of one person on the 'boards,' and, in technical language, is called ' filling the stage.' "

This was about the finishing touch to the preparations, as far as Verisopht was concerned; and leaving the good-natured Hooky Wilder to complete any further arrangements which his experience might suggest, he went to look after his relatives, consisting of his father and mother, and the whole family of brothers and sisters, who had driven ten miles to be present.

The house filled speedily until it was crammed. The tradesmen and working men of Snoozleton, with their wives and children, showed in large numbers, and on one of the front benches was the entire Boomershine family in a fervid state of expectation. There were also nearly all the officers of the regiment, and a goodly gathering of the rank and fashion of the neighbourhood, attracted in a great measure by a rumour that the lecture was to be followed by an entertainment, perhaps an *impromptu* dance, up at the barracks. Occupying the seat of honour, and surrounded by his staff, was Major-General Sir Charles Colley-Whobble, K.C.B. The gallant veteran was cudgelling his brains to keep pace with the times and appear scientific; and directly he had heard of the lecture he had said, "This sort of thing is highly creditable; it must be encouraged. I shall attend;" and had come all the way from the headquarters of the district to do so.

Verisopht took his seat in the midst of his family, and while awaiting the appearance of the gallant lecturer, the stage preparations were surveyed with considerable curiosity. On one side of the screen was a large glazed map of the West Indian Islands, stretched on a frame, and on an adjacent table was laid Captain Calipash's valuable collection of curiosities—a sugar-cane, a preserved scorpion in a medicine bottle, a string of beads known as "Job's tears," two stuffed humming-birds, and a calabash. On the other side of the screen, considerably mystifying Verisopht, was a large map of India, also framed and glazed;

and on another table more choice curiosities —a sandal-wood box, a bamboo drinking cup, a tiger's claw, a grass-work cigar-case, and a wooden Hindoo idol. At the back of the stage were two doors, right and left, both of which were watched with considerable expectation.

Verisopht only watched the right-hand one, for he knew that through a crack thereof the eye of Captain Calipash was fixed upon him, awaiting the preconcerted signal for his entrance. When he considered the feelings of the audience had been wound up to the highest pitch, he was to blow his nose. He blew his nose, and Captain Calipash promptly made his appearance.

A burst of applause greeted him, in the midst of which, to Verisopht's horror, the door on the other side of the screen was opened, and Captain Chutney appeared, bowing low to the audience. Our hero's feelings were those of a signalman when he discovers too late that he has sent a train down a single line up which an express is rattling, and, like one in a horrid dream, he awaited the shock.

"Ah, opens with some lighter business, I see," said Major-General Sir Charles Colley-Whobble; "some little pleasantry in the 'Box and Cox' style, evidently." This idea seemed to be shared by most of the audience, to whom it was a pleasant surprise, and the applause was redoubled.

On this Captains Calipash and Chutney smiled and bowed more than ever, and placed their hands upon their hearts. It was without doubt the proudest moment of their lives. With the exception of Verisopht, a listener for five consecutive minutes had been a luxury neither had known for years. But here were listeners by the hundred, not only ready to listen by the hour, but regularly clamouring for the treat. Each seemed to tread on enchanted ground.

"I wonder if that wretched old Chutney is in the house; if he is he'll have a fit," thought Captain Calipash, with a delicious thrill.

"If that miserable old devil Calipash is looking on he must wish he had been carried off by the yellow Jack long ago," soliloquised Captain Chutney with a chuckle.

Smiling and bowing, they both advanced down the stage on either side of the screen, and as they neared the footlights they converged.

Captain Calipash was just clearing his throat for "Oh, know ye the land of the guava and turtle?" which he had determined upon as a graceful opening to his lecture, and Captain Chutney was still bowing and smiling blandly, when they both cleared the screen and—*touched!*

* * * * *

"Capital! Evidently old stagers! Those starts of astonishment and dismay on either side would have reflected credit on the elder Kean," observed Sir Charles Colley-Whobble, who kept up his position of being the biggest gun in the company by making the most noise. The elder Kean, or the younger Kean, however, might in vain have emulated the demeanour of either of the two gentlemen who now figured on the stage of the Snoozleton Town Hall. The purple peony was pale compared to Captain Chutney, and a piece of chalk would have made a black mark on Captain Calipash's cheeks. The climax of their rivalry had been reached. There was no glossing it over now.

"Contemptible driveller!" said Captain Chutney.

'Bombastic sniveller!" hissed Captain Calipash.

That "resistless spirit of poetry," of which Captain Calipash avowed himself the victim, was strikingly apparent in this retort. There were infinitely more cutting epithets of opprobrium in his vocabulary, which he fain would have used, but to a poet "sniveller" was manifestly, on the spur of the moment, the proper repartee to "driveller."

"Ha, ha! very good! By the living Jingo!" said Sir Charles Colley-Whobble pleasantly; "one would really think they were in a rage. I had no idea, Colonel

Rooteen, that you had so much histrionic talent in the regiment."

"It—it—takes me by surprise, General," said Colonel Rooteen, who was utterly at a loss to know what to make of it all.

"Bombastic sniveller!" repeated Captain Calipash.

Passion had clouded his reason, so he stuck to rhyme.

Now in this country, where the climate is so trying and catarrhic affections so prevalent, "sniveller" should be a term conveying no extraordinary degree of obloquy. Indeed, most people would be inclined to class it as a rather mild term of reproach, if of reproach at all. Not so Captain Chutney. It seemed to exasperate him beyond all bounds. "Deeds, not words," was now his mental battle-cry. Seizing his framed and glazed map, which happened to be the first thing that came to hand, Captain Chutney used it as a clown in a circus uses a paper hoop, and in a trice Captain Calipash found himself up to the neck in Central India. The hint was not lost upon Captain Calipash, and seizing *his* map, the purple head of Captain Chutney suddenly protruded from the midst of the Caribbean Sea.

This was well received by the house, and the applause was deafening.

"The amount of intense reality which they throw into their parts is something marvellous," remarked Mr. Boomershine, as the next moment Calipash's calabash split like a segment shell on the crown of Captain Chutney's head, while Captain Chutney's Hindoo idol whizzed viciously through the air. "A leetle *too* realistic, perhaps," added Mr. Boomershine, as the "Job's tears" beads rattled about his head like a shower of hail, and a shriek from Mrs. Boomershine announced the descent of the preserved scorpion on her neck.

Of all the curiosities, however, none distinguished themselves so much as the Hindoo idol. It just missed Captain Calipash's head, and catching Major-General Sir Charles Colley-Whobble, K.C.B., well between the eyes, just as he was in the very act of saying "Brayvo!" opened those organs in one sense, while it closed them in another.

"Zounds!" roared Sir Charles; "they're in earnest. Turn out the regimental guard! Send them to their rooms under escort; sentries over their doors with side-arms, and loaded with ball-cartridge, by gad!"

"Are you much hurt, sir?" anxiously inquired Sir Charles's aide-de-camp.

"Am I much hurt, sir? Don't be an idiot, or you'll go back to your regimental duty pretty sharp, I can tell you. Am I much hurt, indeed! Try and stop an express train with your head, sir, and ask yourself if you're much hurt. Don't be a fool, sir. Go to the devil!"

"This is a disgraceful scene, sir," said Colonel Rooteen, who of course, as the reader knows, was a first-rate officer, and equal to any emergency. "Don't you think, General, that if my Adjutant were to bring it officially to my notice, and I were to report it to your Adjutant-General, and he were to report it to you, and you were to tell him to tell me to tell my Adjutant to tell them to consider themselves under close arrest, it would be the best course to pursue under the circumstances? Or, perhaps, if I were to embody my report in the form of an official letter and——"

"Confound your official letter, sir!" roared Sir Charles; "I couldn't read it if you were to put it before me. What's an official letter to a man blinded for life by a Hindoo idol in both eyes? Away with them at once! I'll smash them both by court-martial, as sure as my name's Colley-Whobble!"

By this time the rival lecturers had come to close quarters. In the scuffle the screen had fallen over them, and by its violent upheavals the combatants, though lost to sight, were evidently pommelling each other under it. Several of their brother officers now leaped on the stage, and in a few moments Captains Calipash and Chutney were on the way to their quarters in separate flies, each guarded.

The inflamed orb of Colonel Rooteen now rested on Verisopht.

"Aha!" said Colonel Rooteen, starting back, "so young in the service, and yet so guilty of 'conduct to the prejudice of good order and military discipline,' eh!" And Colonel Rooteen bustled up to the General. There was a hurried council of war, the result of which was that Hooky Wilder and Verisopht, as aiders and abettors in the disgraceful transaction, were forthwith ordered off to their rooms under close arrest.

Like an electric shock was the thrill of horror which ran down that particular bench on which the Boomershine family were seated when the dire intelligence of Wilder and Verisopht's arrests reached them. The elders maintained a certain show of outward calm; but the younger members, to whose imagination the step was merely a preliminary to being shot, set up a piteous howl for their unfortunate brother. The double-barrelled grief of the twins, as going off with that simultaneousness which had characterised their appearance, and probably their first howl on life's stage, was peculiarly harrowing. What had been all their little trials compared to this one? What had been a defunct guinea-pig, a squashed silkworm, the orthographical difficulties in connection with cat and dog, compared to a slaughtered brother? Nothing, was evidently their opinion, and they howled as they had never howled before.

Of the whole family, however, that foolish little Fanny suffered the most acutely, and it was with the greatest difficulty that she prevented herself from following the example of her younger brothers and sisters, whose ideas on the subject of military discipline she partially shared. Sisterly affection, however, was not entirely the cause of her agitation. Her grief was "two-edged," and I fear that the sharper edge was that "put on" by consideration for that reprobate Hooky Wilder.

"The meeting," as the local paper said

the following morning, "now broke up in considerable disorder."

* * * * *

Verisopht was kept in durance vile for a short period. At the very first Wilder had tried to explain how free from all blame was his innocent accomplice; but Sir Charles Colley-Whobble and Colonel Rooteen in their then "away-with-them, off-with-their-heads" frame of mind, would listen to nothing. On their arrival in barracks, however, Wilder repeated his exertions on his young friend's behalf with greater success, and Verisopht was forthwith released from arrest to the joy of the Boomershine family, who were weepingly awaiting tidings in a private room of the principal hotel at Snoozleton.

The cases of the other three delinquents were not so easily disposed of. Captains Calipash and Chutney were kept in arrest and suspense for several weeks. They narrowly escaped trial by court-martial on charges of "disgraceful conduct unbecoming the character of officers and gentlemen,"— elastic phrase, embracing anything, from pulling off a door-knocker to knocking down your Colonel. Their cases were left to the decision of the Commander-in-Chief, who, in consideration of their long services and the deep-laid plot to which both had been victims, let them off with severe reprimands, and then transferred them to other regiments.

Whether by chance or whether with a refinement of cruelty shocking in the extreme we know not, but Captain Calipash, the West Indian hero, the Bard of Tobago, was sent to a regiment in India, the vantage-ground of his hated rival; while Chutney, the pride of Hindostan, the caressed of jewelled begums, the slayer of tigers, found himself appointed to a corps serving not only in the West Indies, but in that most hated portion of it, Tobago! Tobago, where "The Tickler" was published!! "The Tickler" in which that abominable trash had appeared!!!

There was no help for it, and from

Southampton they both diverged to their respective destinations.

Hooky Wilder summed up his own case as the "narrowest squeak he had had." In justice to him, we must record that he painted his own share in the transaction in the blackest possible colour, in order to shield poor Calipash and Chutney, who, in reality, had carried the affair to an extreme barely anticipated by him. He was publicly reprimanded in the presence of all the officers, and an assurance was conveyed to him from the Commander-in-Chief that on the very next unfavourable report of him Her Majesty would dispense with his services. In the meantime, he was informed that a cross of the deepest dye and the largest dimensions was placed against his name in His Royal Highness's black book, which meant no leave in the ensuing season, and soldiering in the West Indies or on the coast of Africa on the slightest provocation.

This escapade of Hooky Wilder's not only deprived home society of those two ornaments, Captains Chutney and Calipash, but it also deprived the Queen and the country of the valuable services of that distinguished veteran Sir Charles Colley-Whobble, K.C.B. The following document explains how and wherefore :

" SIR,—I have the honour to request that you will move His Royal Highness the Field Marshal Commanding-in-Chief to be good enough to accept my resignation of the command I now hold. You will oblige me by explaining to His Royal Highness that I am driven to this step by the firm conviction that a military command is no longer a position for a soldier. Against my better judgment I have endeavoured to keep pace with the times. I have been up in a balloon for *reconnaissance* purposes, and remained insensible the whole time owing to the rarity of the atmosphere, only recovering myself as we were descending through a conservatory, for which I had to pay fifty pounds damages, the War Office disallowing my claim for reimbursement. Undeterred from further aeronautic investigation, I again was present at a similar experiment, I remaining on this occasion below, in which position I was first caught by the balloon's grapnel, and hurried across an entire field at a most undignified pace, and then, owing to the imperfect knowledge of his duties possessed by the person throwing out ballast, received a sandbag on my head, which completely destroyed a new cocked-hat, and all but dislocated my neck. The careless way in which this experiment was conducted led to the additional inconvenience of a change of aides-de-camp, I having felt it incumbent upon my position to send the officer then acting in that capacity back to his regimental duties for indulging in ill-restrained mirth whilst detaching the grapnel from my person.

"I next served, you will be good enough to bring to the notice of His Royal Highness, as a member of a committee on

Harbour Defence, and descended in a diving-bell in company with a General of the Royal Engineers and an Admiral, for the purpose of acquainting ourselves with the method of laying torpedoes. Unfortunately while confined in this small space below the surface, my brother General and the Admiral, who were both exceedingly deaf, held different views, and I was drawn up one of them for life, from an auricular point of view. I may here beg to remind His Royal Highness that the committee adopted the views of the Admiral, owing to his having brought his speaking-trumpet with him. The loss of this faculty—for which I have received no compensation, though sustained in the service of my country—occasionally places me, I beg to point out, in extremely false positions, as instanced a short time ago when, attending the trial of the eighty-one ton gun at Shoeburyness, I severely reprimanded my aide-de-camp for his want of manners in sneezing too close to my head, when in point of fact the noise I had attributed to him proceeded from the gun under trial at the moment of explosion.

"I now come to the immediate cause of my secession from the service. While attending a lecture by two officers—which I did with the sole purpose of encouraging science in the army—I have been all but blinded for life by a Hindoo idol, which was used as a missile in a disgraceful scene, of which a full report is transmitted to the Adjutant-General at head-quarters, for the information and consideration of His Royal Highness. It is while smarting under this last injury that I write these words, placing my resignation in the hands of the Field-Marshal Commanding-in-Chief.

"I have the honour to be, Sir,
 "Your most obedient servant,
  "CHARLES COLLEY-WHOBBLE, K.C.B.,

   "*Lieutenant-General commanding the North-East by South District.*

 "To the Military Secretary.
  "To H.R.H. the Field-Marshal
   Commanding-in-Chief, Horse Guards."

* * * * *

Verisopht's tender heart was much wrung by the fates of poor Calipash and Chutney. The latter never quite forgave him, but Calipash took a most tender farewell of him, and with tears in his eyes repeated for the last time his touching little poems about the turtle and the sugar-cane.

"Good-bye, my dear Boomershine," said Calipash. "I have never met, and I shall never meet again, a man with so much soul as you have."

Soul, in Captain Calipash's sense, meant powers of endurance in listening.

Poor Calipash! Verisopht even now often thinks of him in his exile with a sad feeling. In his mind's eye he sees his old friend's sallow, earnest face; on his mind's ear there falls, in the well-remembered tremulous, impassioned tones, the tender inquiry:

"Know ye the land where the guava and turtle," &c.

Then in Verisopht's thoughts the earnest

face brightens up, the eye seems to fire, the mouth to water, and he hears once again in the old rapturous notes :

"Oh, know ye the joys and delights to be got
  From sangaree, cassarceepe, hot pepper-pot?"

CHAPTER XX.

Tardy regeneration of Mentor — Daring trespass — Domestic devotion — The pursuit of botany under touching circumstances — Remorse — The *amende honorable*.

ON so intimate a footing did Wilder establish himself with the Boomershine family that before very long he was made the confidant of the wrong under which it still smarted—the withdrawal of the light of Aunt Millicent's countenance.

"It all originated, my dear Mr. Wilder," said Mr. Boomershine one day, "in the unfortunate prejudice she entertains against your noble profession."

"My dear sir," returned Wilder, "to remove that unfortunate prejudice shall be my aim in life."

Though holding a very exalted opinion of Mr. Wilder's transcendent abilities, Mr. Boomershine shook his head and smiled incredulously.

"Not only," continued Wilder, "shall this prejudice be removed, but I shall give you a tangible proof of the same. I and several of my brother officers shall lunch with Miss Simple, by her own express invitation, before we are two weeks older."

The incredulous smile vanished from Mr. Boomershine's benevolent countenance. Not that he had ceased to be incredulous, but he felt his estimable young friend was raving, and he was pained to see how so noble a mind was here o'erthrown.

For the following week Wilder concentrated all his energies on one point. He not only elicited a great deal of information from the Boomershines concerning Aunt Millicent's habits and customs, but he also reconnoitred in his own person that eccentric lady's premises. Moreover, he was much engaged during this period in certain mysterious preparations in conjunction with sundry young subalterns, who were ever ready to place themselves implicitly under his leadership in any project of his devising.

On a certain forenoon Miss Millicent Simple, accompanied by her maid and a few pets, sat, according to custom, in an arbour in the grounds surrounding the house whither she had fled from the contaminating atmosphere of Snoozleton, when that place had been converted into a military quarter. On the table in the centre of the summer-house was placed Mentor, in his cage, and the work on hand was evidently the regeneration of that fallen bird. Alas! he was but half reclaimed. In the middle of the first bar of the "Old Hundredth" he would suddenly branch off into "Pop goes the Weasel," and an opprobrious epithet was frequently introduced with startling effect into the middle of a moral precept. Whenever he showed symptoms of backsliding in this grievous manner Aunt

Millicent would sharply enjoin the maid to stuff her fingers into her ears; while she herself, with noble steadfastness, stood the broadside of abuse with which Mentor raked her fore and aft. At times the depraved creature nearly blew Aunt Millicent's head off with the strength of his remarks, and it was only by the aid of her smelling-salts and a strong sense of duty that she was able to remain at her post.

It was while Miss Millicent was thus engaged that the maid, whose sense of seeing was perhaps sharpened by the temporary and artificial deprivation of the faculty of hearing, exclaimed:

"Lawks, miss, if here ain't some men coming up the walk! I do believe they're orficers from the barracks at Snoozleton."

"Officers! Barracks! Coming up *my* walk!" gasped Miss Simple in three spasms.

"Yes, miss, that they are. Well, I never! Did *you* ever, miss?"

Thus appealed to, Miss Simple mentally

sought an historical parallel, and finding it in the episode of the Sabine women and the Roman soldiery, shuddered from head to foot.

"Wha-wha-what are they doing?" she asked in tones tremulous with fear and indignation. "They're inebriated of course, and rolling about; and—and I shouldn't wonder if there's going to be a prize-fight, and they've had the audacity to choose this sequestered spot for their brutal purpose—the wretches!"

"No, miss," replied the maid, who kept a sharp and not altogether hostile look-out on the advancing enemy; "they seem quite peaceful. They keep stopping and examining the trees and plants, and writing down something in their note-books, and one of them seems to be lecturing them like."

"Dear me, what *can* they be doing?" said Miss Simple, curiosity for the moment getting the better of fear, and, for the first time since the maid's announcement had spread alarm and horror in her breast, she allowed her eyes to rest on the audacious invaders of her privacy. "Gracious! their movements are certainly most mysterious. They are so wrapt in their occupation, whatever it may be, that I believe we should have time to escape to the house without being seen."

"I think, miss," said the maid, who, during Miss Simple's observation of the foe, had been busily arranging her cap and smoothing her hair, "it would be safer to stay where we are. If they was to see us they'd be sure to run after us and kiss us. It's a way they've got in the army, miss."

"The libertines! the wretches!"

"But if they was to try it, miss, I'd defend you to the last gasp. I'd say, 'Kiss me, 'ug me, do anythink you like, but spare my missis.'"

"Noble girl," murmured Aunt Millicent. "I shall never forget this devotion. I shall follow your advice and stay here."

In silence the approach was now watched. It was slow, owing to constant inexplicable stoppages of the party, and some minutes elapsed before the intruders were within earshot of the summer-house. At this awful juncture Aunt Millicent summoned up all her fortitude to hear the ribald jest or the licentious oath which she had not the slightest doubt was so soon to shatter her notions of propriety to their very foundations. In place, however, of either the one or the other, there fell on her wondering ears, in tones so innocent and bland that the speaker seemed to bleat, the following remark :

"And here, my dear brother-officers, we have a perfect specimen of the *Juniperus Chinensis*, or the Chinese juniper, a cupuliferous shrub, and a native of China, introduced into this country in the year 1804."

On this there was a general and searching examination of the cupuliferous shrub, and sundry notes were taken down by the members of the party.

Aunt Millicent watched and listened spellbound, while the good-looking maid evinced some symptoms of disappointment as the opportunity for displaying the noble self-devotion she had pledged herself to seemed to wane.

"What a beautiful study is botany," continued the one who was evidently the leader of the party; "and to us in a special degree have been vouchsafed opportunities of observing this engrossing science in its loftiest aspects, for who is there amongst us who has not frequently experienced the sensation of being up a tree?"

"Ah, what an elevating thing it is to be up a tree!" observed one of the party.

"It is indeed," murmured several in mild tones.

Aunt Millicent here betrayed symptoms of interest. Repugnance and indignation were gradually fading away from her face, and giving place to attention, not wholly unmixed with admiration.

"And here, again," went on the bleating voice in tones of gentle ecstasy, "is a specimen, a be-a-uti-ful specimen, of the *Fraxinus Excelsior*, or pendulous-branched ash, an *oleaceous* tree, a native of Timbuctoo."

"The erudition he displays is marvellous," murmured Aunt Millicent, whose nose was now protruding through the trellis-work of the arbour in a frenzy of curiosity.

"I am sorry," continued this erudite personage, "that our esteemed young friend Boomershine was unable to accompany us on this little botanical expedition. I should have enjoyed initiating him into those calm joys to be obtained from a contemplation of the *Fraxinus Excelsior*, or pendulous— Aha!" said the speaker, with a sudden transition from the vegetable to the animal kingdom, as one of Aunt Millicent's pets, a fine cat, emerged from the arbour and presented itself in his path; "here we have the *Felis Domesticus*, the domestic cat: order, *Thomasus Tiliensis*."

Aunt Millicent was conquered. The tenderest chords had been touched. She laid down her arms.

"I have been unjust," she murmured. "I have condemned the innocent unheard. As I said before, the erudition he displays is simply wonderful. *Thomasus Tiliensis.* Dear me! I myself, who have studied the subject for years, did not know the particular order of the feline tribe to which this attached creature belongs. *Thomasus Tiliensis!* Beautiful!"

The strangers were now crowding round the domestic animal with tender and soft cries of " Pussy, pussy, poor pussy then."

What a change had come o'er the spirit of Aunt Millicent's dream! The tears of self-reproach filled her eyes, and again she murmured, " I have been unjust. I have wronged the innocent. Dear me, what beautiful sentiments!"

This last remark applied to an oration that was being delivered over the cat.

" What an instance is here afforded us, my dear brother-officers, of the gentle influence exercised by kindness over the most savage natures. Here is an animal by kindness and affection transformed from a tiger into the solace of our firesides. Instead of a roar, striking terror to our hearts, a plaintive 'miaou' appeals tenderly to us."

"Exquisite!" fell from Aunt Millicent in broken accents.

"It's very predatory instincts, which were once directed against man, are now enlisted in his service, for the guardianship of his hearth, and his home, and his larder, against the inroads of 'rats and mice and such small deer,' as our immortal bard says. What evidences of loving care we read in this tasteful blue riband tied round the faithful creature's neck! What —Oh, goodness gracious me!"

"What is it? What has happened to warrant the use of such strong language?" asked one, with considerable reprehension in his tones. "Yes, what *can* have betrayed you into such unwonted warmth of speech?" sternly demanded another; while the remainder shook their heads and turned up their eyes to show how pained and shocked they were.

"And these are the men whose every word I had thought had been an oath," muttered Aunt Millicent, with a bitter pang of remorse.

"I beg your pardon for what is I know unpardonable, but I will explain what led me into these unseemly ejaculations. It is not likely that an animal so well cared for, so lovingly tended as this one evidently is, would stray far from the loving hand which tends to its wants and from the home which shelters it from the inclemency of the weather and the persecutions of boys and of dogs. It was the contemplation of this which suddenly awoke me to the fact that in the excitement of finding a beautiful specimen of the *Viburnum Cassinoides*, the cassine-like viburnum, a cupuliferous shrub, and in the ardour of the subsequent search after more varieties, we have unwittingly been guilty of trespass. These are evidently private grounds."

Blank dismay fell on the party.

"It is not man-traps; it is not steel-guns; it is not prosecution with the utmost rigour of the law that we fear—it is the condemnation of our own consciences."

A general murmur endorsed this noble sentiment, and the party moved as if on the point of beating a precipitate retreat.

At this juncture Miss Millicent Simple would have rushed forward with an invitation to stay on her lips, so completely had the belief of a lifetime been upset by the previous ten minutes. But her heart was too full to speak, and maidenly reserve riveted her to the spot where she sat.

"And yet stay," said the last speaker, as he suddenly arrested the departure of the group. "This tenderly cared for animal as it purrs and rubs itself against our legs gives us a lesson of confidence in human nature. The individual who owns these grounds evidently owns this attached creature, and the individual who owns this attached creature evidently possesses a kind heart, and would, I feel assured, not begrudge us, while we partake of our frugal repast, the grateful shade afforded by these beautiful trees of the cupuliferous and aque-foliaceous orders. Here, my dear companions," said the speaker, producing a bag full of biscuits, "are two Abernethies apiece. We have learned in our boyhood that hunger is the best condiment, but the experiences of manhood prove that there is a still better — an approving conscience. Let us, then, recollect as we eat that this frugality, this rigid economy, is practised in order that out of our scant and inadequate means we may be able to subscribe more fully to the funds of that benevolent society for providing the inhabitants of equatorial Africa with double-breasted Ulsters and warming-pans."

Miss Millicent Simple could stand no more. The icy barrier of maidenly reserve, already considerably thawed, melted away altogether before the glowing picture of peace presented by an inhabitant of equatorial Africa with a double-breasted Ulster and a warming-pan.

"Go," she said to the pretty maid; "go," she exclaimed, with streaming eyes and in agitated tones. "Go to the house and tell them to prepare the best luncheon that the larder affords; and tell Binns to get out some Madeira — *the*

Madeira, mind. Quick; do not lose a moment."

As the maid rushed to obey this behest, Miss Millicent Simple emerged from the arbour, and presented herself to the strangers.

The tableau is here left where tableaux often are when the writer feels he cannot do them justice — to the imagination of the reader.

In a quarter of an hour Hooky Wilder's boast to Mr. Boomershine, that he and a party of brother-officers would lunch with Miss Millicent Simple, was being fulfilled.

CHAPTER XXI.

A *reconnaissance*—Joe Miller in regimentals — The game of war — A picture of peace — Colonel Rooteen's brain reels under a shock—He recovers—Villany exposed—A rapid retrograde movement.

"NOW, Boomershine, it is as a Snoozleshire man that I have got you to accompany my Adjutant and myself on this—this *reconnaissance*, I may call it. I feel it is my duty to make myself thoroughly acquainted with the strategical features of the locality, and your knowledge of the country may be of service."

Thus spake Colonel Rooteen as, accompanied by Lieutenant Dressop, his Adjutant, and Verisopht Boomershine, he walked along a country road in a remote corner of Snoozleshire, towards which they had all three just journeyed by train.

"By the way, though," said Colonel Rooteen, "you say you do not know very much of this neighbourhood?"

"No, sir," replied Verisopht. "I have an aunt who has lately come somewhere about here, but—but—"

"Ah," interrupted Colonel Rooteen, "I detect a certain amount of hesitation. You had better embody your reply in the form of an official letter, and send it on through the proper channel, and—dear me, dear me, I mean I have heard all about it—antipathy to soldiers, retreated before the enemy on our arrival at Snoozleton, and all that sort of thing. The cultivation of friendly intercourse with the inhabitants is laid down in a military maxim of considerable antiquity, and I hope that by a careful observance of the rule this unfortunate prejudice may be speedily removed. Now, Boomershine, when right's in front what's the pivot?" suddenly asked Colonel Rooteen, putting his favourite rudimentary question by way of freshening up Verisopht's military genius before commencing the topographical examination of that young officer.

"I beg your pardon, sir, that's obsolete," said the Adjutant.

"Never mind, Boomershine," said Colonel Rooteen; "I'll ask you something harder. And I *do* wish, Mr. Dressop, you would endeavour to keep pace with the times. I admit that the frequent alterations and changes in our system of drill are extremely puzzling; but you must march along, sir, with the requirements of the age. You must not halt; you must not mark time. If you do, you'll—you'll—by gad, sir, you'll be left behind."

Here Colonel Rooteen's demeanour suddenly altered, and his countenance became like an April sky alternately bright and clouded, and through all these changes of expression he kept on muttering to himself, "Left behind—dear me, it's *somewhere*." At last, to continue the meteorological metaphor, the sun shone brightly forth and the clouds disappeared below the horizon.

"Mr. Dressop, sir," said Colonel Rooteen in a burst of chuckles, "if right's in front you'll be left behind. Ha, ha, ha!"

This was a joke, and a very fair specimen of Colonel Rooteen's jokes, which always had such a fine old "shoppy" flavour about them that it required about thirty years' service in the army, with a close attention to details, before a person could thoroughly understand and appreciate them. As our readers will not be composed mainly of field-marshals we abstain from drawing to any great extent on Colonel Rooteen's fund of humour.

"Now," he remarked, suddenly arresting his steps opposite the well-kept grounds of a comfortable-looking house; "what a capitally built residence that would be for defensive purposes, supposing of course that your enemy was not able to bring up his artillery. Those wings and projections would admit of such a capital flanking fire.

"Now, Boomershine, what would you do if you had to hold that house with, say, a company of men, and the enemy within a day's march of you? Well, well, perhaps that is a little too advanced for you just yet, and so we'll enlighten you. The first thing would be to cut down all the surrounding trees and shrubs which might afford cover to the enemy."

"Using the boughs and smaller branches for *abattis*," said the Adjutant.

"Blow up the stables and all the out-houses," said the Colonel, gradually working himself up into an apoplectic condition.

"Demolish that summer-house," said the Adjutant ruthlessly.

"Take out all the windows, and fill them up with sand-bags," said the Colonel in quite a martial glow.

"Leaving space enough between them to serve as loopholes," added the Adjutant excitedly.

"Or if sand-bags aren't available, use the mattresses and bedding," spluttered the Colonel, with his eyes starting out of his head. The game of war was getting terribly exciting.

"Or the doors taken off their hinges, and the tables and sofas," said the Adjutant, with the keenest interest.

"Or, by gad, if that wouldn't do," said the Colonel, his utterance almost choked by the torrent of expedients with which his inflamed military brain was overflowing, "I'd shoot the men-servants and the maid-servants and the cattle and every confounded stranger within the gates, and use their bodies as sand-bags. Nothing should beat *me*, by gad! And, and—well I don't think there would be anything more to do then, Mr. Dressop, except to keep a sharp look-out and your powder dry, eh?" said the Colonel, after a pause, and as he wiped from his brow the perspiration engendered by the heat with which he had thrown himself into the exciting topic.

"Nothing more, sir; I don't think we omitted anything of importance."

"I think, Mr. Dressop, we conducted the

defence of that post with a tolerable amount of ability?"

"Yes, sir; most certainly so. That sand-bag expedient, in particular, was undoubtedly brilliant, sir."

"Well, well, I will not say that as a *dernier ressort* it has not some merits. In that comfortable-looking establishment the butler, I'll be bound, is a sort of fellow who could be converted into a most efficient sand-bag. "Imperial Cæsar, dead and turned to clay, may stop a hole to keep the *shot* away"—with all apologies to Shakespeare, for whose military genius I have the greatest respect. He was a thorough soldier at heart, sir, if not by profession. But enough of this digression. Let us reverse the 'general idea.' And, dear me, what a delightful afternoon we *are* having! Let us suppose ourselves the attacking force, say, with a wing of the regiment. Now, Boomershine, pay great attention. I shall give you as practical a lesson as possible. The first thing I should do, of course, would be to reconnoitre.

Now, the great principle in reconnoitring is to see as much while being seen as little as possible. I therefore," said Colonel Rooteen, as he crept stealthily behind a tender sapling of about an inch and a half in diameter, " take advantage of cover, that is, conceal myself. Thus effectually concealed," continued Colonel Rooteen, as he peered cautiously beyond the tender sapling with the air of a Sioux Indian on the war trail, " I proceed to—to—dear me ! What the dickens is the meaning of that ?"

Colonel Rooteen then looked at the Adjutant, who looked at Verisopht, who gazed in utter bewilderment at a group which suddenly came into view round a turning of one of the walks in the private grounds. The group numbered about five or six persons, and the two most conspicuous figures were an elderly lady and a young man. The elderly lady leaned upon the young man's arm, and seemed to hang on every word that fell from his lips, while the young man, with a subdued and deeply-contemplative cast of countenance, seemed to be expatiating in terms of great eloquence, to judge from the admiration and delight on the lady's face, on the surrounding beauties of nature. One of the young gentlemen comprising the group carried in his arms a sleek cat, which ever and anon he stroked with a tenderness bespeaking a deep affection for the species; while another bore with equal solicitude and care a lapdog somewhat inclined to *embonpoint*. Altogether, the party presented a picture of peaceful and innocent harmony seldom seen in this world of strife and envy.

As Verisopht Boomershine gazed he gasped out, "Aunt Millicent!"

"Hooky Wilder!" ejaculated the Adjutant.

"I hardly believe my senses," murmured Colonel Rooteen. "It is some day-dream, some phantom of the brain. I once had a sunstroke in India and a sabre wound on the head, and between the two," faltered the poor gentleman, "I may be wandering in my mind. Or this wild fancy may be the result of a disordered system. I have certainly," continued Colonel Rooteen, in feeble tones, "experienced of late a dizziness of sight and a tightness across the head; I shall make my Adjutant take a four-grained blue-pill to-night, and the sergeant-major a saline draught in the morning. For if one has a disagreeable duty before one, what the deuce is the good of having subordinates if you can't make them perform it for you? I don't know though," he added, as the mind gradually reasserted itself; "I fear in this case there would be a missing link in the chain of responsibility. No, no, this is no fancy. There is some mischief brewing—certain to be wherever that young scamp is—and it is my duty at once to expose him."

At this point Aunt Millicent espied Verisopht, while simultaneously Wilder and his fellow-conspirators caught sight of their commanding-officer. For the first time in his life Hooky Wilder looked, as well as felt, disconcerted. But this was only a momentary weakness. Suddenly remembering, on the part of himself and friends, a pressing engagement which would not admit of one instant's delay, he and they took their departure, in spite of Miss Millicent Simple's earnest entreaties to stay while in their presence she made the *amende honorable* to her nephew and Colonel Rooteen. As Wilder and his companions precipitately retreated in one direction, Colonel Rooteen, accompanied by Verisopht, advanced in the other.

For a few moments Miss Simple paused to gaze on the retreating form of Hooky Wilder, and then pressed forward to meet her young relative.

"Verisopht, my dear boy," she exclaimed, as she fell on his neck, "I have been unjust. I have maligned your noble profession; but now my eyes have been opened. Is that Colonel Rooteen? Introduce me. I shall esteem his acquaintance a great honour."

"Madam," said Colonel Rooteen, lifting his hat and ramming it on his head again very fiercely, "I am glad to hear that your sentiments concerning the profession I belong to have undergone a change; but the society I saw you in, under circumstances so strange and unaccountable that for a few moments I believed myself to be dreaming, renders it probable, madam, that your present good opinion of us is formed on as false a foundation as your former bad one was. Madam, I apprehend that you have been the victim of a hoax."

"Oh, impossible!" gushed Miss Millicent Simple; "he could not be guilty of such a thing. Such beautiful language, such a true appreciation of the beauties of nature, such an ardent admirer of domestic animals—no, he could not deceive!"

"It strikes me forcibly, madam, that he not only can, but that he has just done so."

"Then he is not what he said he was?" asked Miss Millicent in broken accents.

"Did he say, madam, that he was the biggest young scamp in the regiment; that he was a thorn in the side of good order and military discipline, so to speak; that he had been expelled from the Staff College; that he is, in short, a young rascal from whose knavish tricks neither sex nor age nor rank is safe?"

"No, no."

"Then, madam, to use affirmatively the words you put interrogatively, 'Then he is not what he said he was.'"

"And you, you," said Miss Millicent, betraying symptoms of approaching hysterics, "are not what he said *you* were? You do not belong to the society for providing the inhabitants of equatorial Africa with double-breasted Ulster coats and—"

"Oh, pooh!" ejaculated Colonel Rooteen, blowing out his cheeks, and purpling under the aspersion on his character. "Just like the young rascal's impudence. I belong, madam, to a society for providing the inhabitants of Africa with a bullet in their interior whenever we come across 'em. *That's* the society *I* belong to, madam."

The impending fit of hysterics here broke forth, and Aunt Millicent's shrieks speedily brought an excited crowd of female servants to the rescue. In the van of the domestics was an inflamed-looking cook, armed with a spit; and amongst the rest such weapons of feminine warfare as flatirons, curling-tongs, &c., were freely brandished.

"Egad!" said Colonel Rooteen as Miss Millicent's shrieks of "Go away! Oh, go away, you wretches!" incited the approaching throng to greater rapidity and fury. "Egad! appearances are deucedly against one. There's no knowing of what I may be accused. Mr. Dressop, sir, you'll be good enough to create a diversion from a retrograde movement on the part of the main body by tumbling into that horsepond. Possibly they may stop to pick you out; probably they will not; but at all events they are certain to pause to enjoy the spectacle. If you're drowned I'll take all responsibility off your shoulders."

By "main body" Colonel Rooteen, of course, alluded to his own, as was only right, seeing that it weighed rather more than the other two put together; and having thus taken precautions for covering its retreat, he proceeded to execute a retrograde movement of considerable celerity.

From a fir plantation not one hundred yards away, Hooky Wilder watched the evolution with aching sides and streaming eyes.

CONCLUSION.

Satisfactory, we hope, to all concerned.

THOUGH not, as may be gathered from the conclusion of the last chapter, by any means insensible to the exquisite enjoyment afforded by the spectacle of his commanding-officer fleeing from the wrath of an excited throng of females, Wilder was still considerably chagrined at the unexpected *dénouement* resulting from Colonel Rooteen's military observation of the surrounding country. Aunt Millicent's conversion through his (Wilder's) means would have been a triumph which would have placed him at the zenith of popularity with the Boomershines, with whom, for obvious reasons, he was particularly anxious to stand well; but now he felt that, instead of filling up the breach between the estranged relatives, he had widened and deepened it to an extent which in all probability could never be bridged over, and that the whole affair had turned out a miserable *fiasco*, of which the least said the better. This last view of the case was not the one taken by Colonel Rooteen. It was many days before Wilder heard the last of it. "Reasons in writing," "wiggings" in the orderly-room, threats of courts-martial, were a few of the terrors Colonel Rooteen held over the delinquent. But through this dangerous sea, teeming with shoals and rocks, Wilder steered his bark with consummate skill into calmer waters.

In the meantime our hero Verisopht Boomershine had ceased to occupy that lowly position known as "boots;" that is to say, he was no longer the junior officer of the regiment. Another sub-lieutenant had joined, and Verisopht proudly felt that he now had his foot firmly planted on the first step of the ladder leading up to the field-marshal's bâton. Altogether, he was getting well into the swing of a military career, when a letter from Aunt Millicent threw him into a state of indecision and doubt. It ran thus:

"DEAR VERISOPHT,

"Tormentor, as, alas! I must still call him, not only steadily refuses to turn over a new leaf, but has also corrupted a once virtuous bird whose society I had hoped would have reformed him. The readiness with which both have picked up what was wicked, compared with their very gradual acquirement of what was good, is to me an unmistakable proof of the natural proneness to evil of their species. I am thus thoroughly convinced that my reformatory home for soldiers' and sailors' parrots and my project for the regeneration of Africa would be failures, and have consequently abandoned those schemes. I have now quite lost faith in these animals, and I find that I must give something else a place in my affections. I need not tell you that, after the visit of that viper and his noisome brood, the army, of which they are indeed fitting members, is to me, if possible, more hateful than ever. If you will give it up, and thus throw off the yoke which Satan has placed on your neck, and fill up the void in my heart caused by Tormentor's backsliding, I shall make you a handsome allowance during my lifetime, and constitute you my sole heir at my decease. I shall give you a week to decide, and in the meantime I remain your anxious and expectant aunt,

"Millicent Simple."

With strange infatuation Verisopht appealed to Wilder for counsel, and that individual, after reading the letter and muttering something about "hatters" and "March hares," advised him to "close with the old girl's offer and chuck the service."

"Anyhow," he added, "you must consult your people, and I'll drive you over this very afternoon."

They drove over, and the letter threw the family into a bewildering state of perplexity. Mr. Boomershine was loath to deprive the country of a future Wellington; but at the same time he was not blind to the superior advantages of a bird in the hand over one in the bush, and he wavered. So hard was it to know what to do, that at last it was decided to take advantage of the entire week offered by Aunt Millicent before settling the knotty point.

The week had nearly passed, and Verisopht was still tossing on a sea of doubt, when Wilder came to him one morning with a letter in his hand.

"I say, Boomershine, here's a queer coincidence! They want me to leave the service too. Had a letter from the governor this morning. Here's what the old boy says:

"'DEAR REGINALD,

"'I have heard of your last escapade. I am sick and tired of this nonsense, and foresee that, sooner or later, if left to your own devices, you will disgrace your family by being publicly dismissed from the service.'

"That's what I call precious cool, considering that the old boy was kicked out of the army himself, when he was a youngster, for painting his colonel's charger sky-blue," interpolated Wilder. "It must be congenital, and it's very ungenerous casting what one can't help into one's teeth. He might as well abuse me for inheriting his Roman nose. I rather like *this* part of his letter though :

"'Now I'm convinced that there is nothing like matrimony for steadying a young man, if the choice be a wise one; and if you could come across some modest unsophisticated young girl—none of your garrison hacks, mind you, that you young fellows sometimes get hooked by, but an innocent well-brought-up young lady that you could love, I should be only too glad to see you married and settled down, and I would receive her with open arms. She need not have much money. Let her be all I have described, and that will do. I am lonely in this country-house by myself, and you could live here just as you would do after my death. Your uncle, to whom I've spoken on the subject, told me that, if you married as I wished, he would again alter his will to its original form, in your favour, as it stood before you were expelled from the Staff College. Think well of all this. Never mind about the money, I repeat. Your mother brought me no other dowry than modesty, virtue, and a loving heart; and never was man richer than I in the possession of these. That is a dream of the past now, my dear boy, and all I have to look forward to is to see you enjoying a happiness similar to that which was once mine.

"'Your affectionate father,
"'R. C. Wilder.'"

Verisopht noticed that Wilder, notwithstanding all his recklessness and fun, looked quite serious as he folded up the letter and muttered softly, "Poor old governor, I'm afraid I haven't been exactly a crown of joy to him."

Hooky Wilder, however, was not much given to the melting mood, and by the time the letter was once more in its envelope he was himself again.

"I say, Boomershine, do you know any unsophisticated modest little girl answering to the governor's description, eh?"

"Well, let's see. There are—" And Verisopht began running over the names of numerous Snoozleshire young ladies.

"No; none of those are up to the mark. Suppose you begin where charity does—at home?"

Verisopht looked hopelessly idiotic. Somehow the possibility of a sister marrying seldom enters the calculations of a brother until the fact is fired off point-blank under his very nose.

"How would you like me for a brother-in-law, old boy?"

"Dear me, do you mean to say—"

"Yes, of course I do. And what's

more, it will be all plain-sailing now. The only difficulty before was that interview with the governor in the study. But now, armed with that letter, I'll beard the lion in his den this very day."

Verisopht, as soon as he had got over his surprise, seized Wilder's hand, and went through a pump-handle performance until he was quite out of breath.

"I wish I could make up my mind what to do about my aunt's letter as easily as you have about your father's," said Verisopht, when the hand-shaking was over.

"Well, my dear Boomershine," said Wilder, "as, at the present rate of promotion, you will be just about one hundred and twenty-five by the time you become a general, I'd advise you to give up the field-marshal's bâton *in futuro* for the 'handsome allowance' *in esse*."

Wilder's counsel, as was always the case, had great weight with Verisopht, and finally, after much heart-burning, he decided on accepting his aunt's offer.

So here was an end of all those dreams

of martial glory in which Verisopht Boomershine had indulged in his quiet country home. And so end the dreams of many a young traveller as he starts on his journey along the road to fame; and for just as miserable a little trifle as the whim of a half-witted old lady, many a dreamer might think with a sigh, when years have passed over his head, and he looks back on the contemptibly small sunken rock on which his bark, dancing gaily along before favourable gales, suddenly went to pieces.

THE END.

BILLING AND SONS, PRINTERS, GUILDFORD.
J. D. & Co.

MISCELLANEOUS SIX-SHILLING VOLUMES.

Each Volume to be had separately, with the exceptions shown, in crown 8vo, cloth, price 6s.

The Autobiography of a Seaman.† 6s.
Madame Campan's Private Life of Mary Antoinette.† 6s.
Renan's Studies in Religious History. 6s.
Cooper's Islands of the Pacific.† 6s.
The Autobiography of Edmund Yates.† 6s.
The Sporting Life of the Rev. "Jack" Russell.† 6s.
Mitford's Recollections of a Literary Life.† 6s.
Brinsley Richards' Seven Years at Eton. 6s.
Low's Life of Lord Wolseley.† 6s.
Bishop Thirlwall's Letters to a Friend.† 6s.
W. H. Mallock's Social Equality. 6s.
W. H. Mallock's Atheism and the Value of Life. 6s.
Arnold's Turning Points in Life. 6s.
The Ingoldsby Legends.† 6s.
Ashley's Life of Lord Palmerston.† 2 vols. 12s.
Stephen's Life of Dean Hook.† 6s.
The Life of the Rev. R. H. Barham (Thomas Ingoldsby).† 6s.
Sir E. Creasy's Fifteen Decisive Battles. 6s.
Sir E. Creasy's History of the English Constitution. 6s.
The Midland Railway.† 6s.
Guizot's Life of Oliver Cromwell.† 6s.
Mignet's Life of Mary Queen of Scots.† 6s.
Barham's Life of Theodore Hook. 6s.
Baker's Our Old Actors.† 6s.
Havard's The Dead Cities of the Zuyder Zee.† 6s.
Timbs' Lives of Painters.† 6s.
Timbs' Lives of Statesmen.† 6s.
Timbs' Wit and Humourists.† 2 vols. 12s.
Timbs' Doctors and Patients. 6s.
The Letters of Runnymede. 6s.
The Bentley Ballads. 6s.
Lady Herbert's Wives & Mothers in the Olden Time. 6s.
W. P. Frith's (R.A.) Autobiography & Reminiscences. 6s.
The New Book of Sports and Games. 6s.
Wood's Cruise of the Reserve Squadron.† 6s.
Wood's In the Black Forest.† 6s.
Letters from Hell. 6s.

† These Volumes contain Portraits, Illustrations, or Maps.

To be obtained at all Booksellers'.

LONDON:
RICHARD BENTLEY & SON, NEW BURLINGTON STREET.
Publishers in Ordinary to Her Majesty the Queen.

BENTLEY'S FAVOURITE NOVELS.

Each work can be had separately, price 6s., of all Booksellers in Town or Country.

By Rhoda Broughton.
Cometh up as a Flower.
Good-bye, Sweetheart.
Joan. | Nancy.
Not Wisely but too Well.
Red as a Rose is She.
Second Thoughts.
Belinda.
'Doctor Cupid.'

By Mrs. Alexander.
The Wooing o't.
Her Dearest Foe.
Look before you Leap.
The Admiral's Ward.
The Executor.
The Freres.
Which Shall it Be?

By Anthony Trollope.
The Three Clerks.

By Marcus Clarke.
For the Term of his Natural Life.

By Hawley Smart.
Breezie Langton.

By Hector Malot.
No Relations.
(With Illustrations.)

By Rosa N. Carey.
Nellie's Memories.
Barbara Heathcote's Trial.
Not like Other Girls.
Only the Governess.
Queenie's Whim.
Robert Ord's Atonement.
Uncle Max.
Wee Wifie.
Wooed and Married.
(See note below.)

By W. E. Norris.
Thirlby Hall.
A Bachelor's Blunder.
Major and Minor.
The Rogue.
(See note below.)

By Mrs. Annie Edwardes.
Ought We to Visit Her?
Leah: a Woman of Fashion.
A Ball-room Repentance.
A Girton Girl.

By Charles Reade.
A Perilous Secret.

By Hon. Lewis Wingfield.
Lady Grizel.

By Mrs. Augustus Craven.
A Sister's Story. *(Reprinting.)*

*** "ARDATH," by MARIE CORELLI, and "SIR CHARLES DANVERS," have just been added to the Series. "HERIOT'S CHOICE," by ROSA NOUCHETTE CAREY, and "MISS SHAFTO,' by W. E. NORRIS, are now in the Press.

LONDON:
RICHARD BENTLEY & SON, NEW BURLINGTON STREET.
Publishers in Ordinary to Her Majesty the Queen.

BENTLEY'S FAVOURITE NOVELS.

Each work can be had separately, price 6s., of all Booksellers in Town or Country.

By Marie Corelli.
A Romance of Two Worlds.
Vendetta!
Thelma.
Ardath.

By Florence Montgomery.
Misunderstood.
Thrown Together.
Seaforth.

By E. Werner.
Success: and how he won it.
Under a Charm.
Fickle Fortune.
No Surrender.

By J. Sheridan Le Fanu.
Uncle Silas.
In a Glass Darkly.
The House by the Churchyard.

By Mrs. Notley.
Olive Varcoe.

By Frances M. Peard.
Near Neighbours.

Anonymous.
The Last of the Cavaliers.
Sir Charles Danvers.

By Lady G. Fullerton.
Ellen Middleton.
Ladybird.
Too Strange not to be True.

By Jessie Fothergill.
The "First Violin."
Borderland.
Healey.
Kith and Kin.
Probation.

By Helen Mathers.
Comin' thro' the Rye.
Sam's Sweetheart.

By Henry Erroll.
An Ugly Duckling.

By Mrs. Parr.
Adam and Eve.
Dorothy Fox.

By Baroness Tautphœus.
The Initials.   Quits!

By Mrs. Riddell.
George Geith of Fen Court.
Berna Boyle.

By Jane Austen.
(Messrs. Bentleys' are the only *complete* Editions of Miss Austen's Works.)
Emma.
Lady Susan, and,
          The Watsons.
Mansfield Park.
Northanger Abbey, and,
          Persuasion.
Pride and Prejudice.
Sense and Sensibility.

LONDON:
RICHARD BENTLEY & SON, NEW BURLINGTON STREET.
Publishers in Ordinary to Her Majesty the Queen.

"One can never help enjoying Temple Bar."—*Guardian.*

THE TEMPLE BAR MAGAZINE.

ONE SHILLING MONTHLY,

Of all Booksellers in the United Kingdom.

"WHO does not welcome **Temple Bar**?"—*John Bull.*

"**Temple Bar** is never without a host of attractive papers."—*Land and Water.*

"**Temple Bar** never flags."—*Standard.*

"**Temple Bar** very happily unites the best contents of the magazine as it was known and flourished a decade and more ago, with the features which readers demand in the modern review."—*Sporting and Dramatic News.*

"**Temple Bar** is just the thing. The articles are short, chatty, and various."—*Examiner.*

"**Temple Bar** is above all things readable."—*St. James's Gazette.*

"**Temple Bar** has a perennial wealth of fiction."—*Graphic.*

"**Temple Bar** has been for several years one of the best of the monthlies."—*Manchester Courier.*

"**Temple Bar** is always delightful reading."—*Life.*

"**Temple Bar** always contains something fresh and interesting."—*Inverness Courier.*

"**Temple Bar** is our favourite magazine."—*Hereford Times.*

"**Temple Bar**.—Brightness and raciness is its normal condition."—*Sheffield Daily Telegraph.*

"**Temple Bar**.—This favourite magazine for town and country readers."—*Burnley Express.*

"**Temple Bar** is as readable as ever."—*Manx Sun.*

"**Temple Bar** has scarcely a dull page in it."—*Birmingham Daily Gazette.*

"**Temple Bar** is remarkably strong in fiction."—*Public Opinion.*

Temple Bar always contains two or more serial stories by first-rate writers.

Temple Bar contains short stories complete in each number.

Temple Bar contains brief chatty biographies of interesting people.

Temple Bar contains light readable articles on subjects of literary, artistic, and general interest.

LONDON:

RICHARD BENTLEY & SON, NEW BURLINGTON STREET.

Publishers in Ordinary to Her Majesty the Queen.

www.ingramcontent.com/pod-product-compliance
Lightning Source LLC
Chambersburg PA
CBHW030802230426
43667CB00008B/1027